"It's truly refreshi[ng] the intersection of a purpose-[filled] on. Dr. Merary Simeon holds on to her principles and moral compasa as a key motivator to climb the corporate ladder. In her continued work, she embraces the light inside her to inspire and share her faith for women to be fearless in their journey."

–Terry Ellis
Founding Member of Legendary Singing Group En Vogue

We are blooming seeds of bitterness
if we aren't focused on
healing.
Everything you went thru had a purpose
in getting you to where you are today.

Regent University
Strategic Leadership.
Isiah 61

H.E.R.A.C.T.

It is sold with the understanding that the publisher and the individual
authors are not engaged in the rendering of psychological, legal,
accounting or other professional advice. The content and views in
each chapter are the sole expression and opinion of its author and not
necessarily the views of Fig Factor Media, LLC.

For more information, contact:
Fig Factor Media, LLC I www.figfactormedia.com

Cover Design by DG Marco Álvarez
Layout by LDG Juan Manuel Serna Rosales

Printed in the United States of America

ISBN: 978-1-7324916-3-2
Library of Congress Control Number: 2022908602

H.E.R.A.C.T.

Activate Your Power. Unlock Your Potential.
Fulfill Your Purpose.

DR. MERARY SIMEON

Dedication

To Team Simeon: my husband Paul, our daughter Neryah and our son Paul Marcel. May the power, potential, and purpose in you always shine bright.

TABLE OF CONTENTS

ACKNOWLEDGMENTS

First of all, I want to give God the glory for giving me the vision for H.E.R.A.C.T. and the endurance to complete this project.

A special thanks to my husband Paul for having my back, standing by me, and supporting my dreams. Thank you for your prayers when I was too tired to write. Thank you for your love and patience through this process. Thank you for slowing me down, reminding me what matters most, and checking when my cup was running empty. Your love makes me better.

Mami and Papi, I love you. Thank you for taking the kids early in the morning on the weekends because you knew I was up writing all night. I know you worried about my late nights writing and would complain you had not seen me sit down to eat a meal in a long time. Yet, you did what was best for me; you prayed for my health, strength, and wisdom so that I could finish strong. Thank you, Mami and Papi, for teaching me that the same power that rose Jesus from the dead lives in me, and through Him, I can do all things.

Without the presence of my dearest friends, Aida and Wendy, I could not imagine my life. You have been there through my heartaches, failures, distance, joy, and successes. You have dropped everything not only to be present but to stay up late working with me to ensure the success of the H.E.R.A.C.T. conferences. When I told you the vision for my book cover, you quickly helped me calm the noise and brought the book cover to life. Thank you for being my pillars. Thank you for your love and unconditional support.

To Monique, thank you. You were the brains behind the

creation of the letters behind the framework. From the moment I told you the idea, you were all in and took the time to think through different ideas. You inspired me to become an author with Radical Woman. Thank you for your ongoing upport. I will forever be grateful to you.

To my trainer, Debbie, thank you for pushing me and ensuring I stayed focused on my physical well-being and for going above and beyond and reading and editing my first manuscript draft. Thank you for the early morning brainstorming sessions on the different chapters. Thank you for helping me live the Simeon motto "stronger than yesterday" during a time when it would have been easy to lose myself. I am stronger mentally and physically because you pushed me to stay focused on my health.

To my daughter Neryah and son Marcel, you have no idea how you inspire me. Thank you for creating your own stories and books because you wanted to be like mommy. Thank you for reminding me how much you love me and how proud you are of me each day. Your make-belief book sales, love, pictures, and words kept me going. Neryah, thank you, my princess, for the beautiful song you wrote. I am proud to showcase it in this book. I know the world will love it as much as I do.

Thank you to Dr. Judy Williams for listening to God's voice, picking up the phone, and calling me every time I needed that nudge that only Dr. Williams can give. For you, I am grateful.

PREFACE

Have you ever had a burning desire to be provided a roadmap to achieving and sustaining your fullest potential? Or perhaps you desire a constant alert that can give clear direction as you chart the course of your life? Yet, before taking off on the journey, you immediately obsess over the non-existent failure?

Have you ever questioned your success and God's blessings bestowed upon you, even when you have worked hard to achieve where you are? If so, this book is for you. H.E.R.A.C.T. provides you with the framework to enable you to stop questioning your value.

H.E.R.A.C.T. is a true page turn, and the H.E.R.A.C.T. framework is clutch! It will feed your soul and encourage the magic in you to be fully present and confident in spaces where you belong. H.E.R.A.C.T. will allow you to reclaim agency, celebrate your achievements, and stop minimizing your personal and professional success as a fluke.

By reading H.E.R.A.C.T., you will gain the tools to say, "I am worthy because I'm here. I am a child of God, and my dedication and obedience have made me who I am." Sis…step into your power and know that God uniquely designed you.

H.E.R.A.C.T. is a great tool to remind you of the importance of unlearning and embracing that healing is an ongoing practice. H.E.R.A.C.T. is an excellent reminder to be brave and aware that you may fall. But when you do…fail forward.

By learning the H.E.R.A.C.T. framework, you will gain the internal ability to relish more in the joy of being up and learning something new. H.E.R.A.C.T. will encourage you to try new things with confidence, invest in what you like, and embrace it with excitement.

H.E.R.A.C.T. is a call to action to all women and our brave co-conspirators to embrace your internal compass and focus on activating your power, unlocking your potential, and fulling your purpose. Know that through Christ, all things are possible. So, activate all that is uniquely you because YOU possess limitless possibilities.

Matthew 25:23: "Well done, good and faithful servant; you have been faithful over a few things; I will make you ruler over many things. Enter into the joy of your lord."

Monique E. Lanaux
Chief Talent & Diversity Officer

A Note from Dr. Merary Simeon

"Do not quench the Spirit."
1 Thessalonians 5:19

As I was writing my dissertation about women in corporate America, I heard a loud voice say, "Healing." It was at that moment God revealed to me the meaning of Healing, Elevation, Respect, Achieve, Confidence, and Transformation (H.E.R.A.C.T.). You see, everything I had experienced in life had prepared me for a time like this. At that moment, I needed to make a difficult decision. Do I re-start my dissertation and serve women? Or do I fulfill my need to finish the dissertation and prove what so many before me have established; there needs to be a change in corporate America.

I chose to serve you. I chose to create a world where women activate their power, unlock their potential, and fulfill their purpose. I believe we can all activate the strength and power that lives within us. I want to share the secrets to removing the obstacles keeping us from God's promises.

I remember calling my chair and explaining how God had other plans for my dissertation. I explain that women are natural leaders; they possess the power within and need to activate it. I want to make a difference; I want to empower women and create a world where the norm is women walking in their power. I want to focus on activating the power we already possess inside us. Once we activate our God-given talents, we are limitless, and the world's rejections will not be able to stop us from achieving greatness. To my surprise, the chair said, "It is a fundamental topic too many people do not talk about; you have my support."

I began my research, and book after book, paper after paper H.E.R.A.C.I. was undeniable. H.E.R.A.C.T. is transformational.

Transformation is what I believe is needed. We can have money, education, and all the things the world has to offer. But if we are not transformed from the inside out, peace will never exist in our lives. We could never enjoy the fruits of our labor living in torment. I lived it (more on this later), and I do not ever want to visit that horrible place again. No, thank you. Now, I'm on a mission to empower every woman around the world. The same power that rose Jesus from the dead lives within me, lives within you, and we must stop muting its power in us. It is not about religion or spirituality. It is about accepting the fact the power of the Holy Spirit lives within us.

As you read H.E.R.A.C.T.., my hope is you'll take in the words and be inspired to act in order to transform your life. With that in mind, you'll find four topics repeated throughout the book:

- Spiritual connection
- Practical exercise
- Ask yourself

When you encounter these sections, I encourage you to pause, read them, and then read them again. In fact, keeping your favorite journal next to you would serve you well. Writing down your thoughts all in one place leads to even greater transformation through the power of the written word.

There is urgency. The world needs the talents you possess. It is time for self-revolution. It's time to remove the obstacles suppressing the power within us. It is time to arise and shine because you are worth the fight!

Chapter 1:

THE H.E.R.A.C.T. FRAMEWORK

"The greatest source of suffering is the lies we tell ourselves."

~ Elvin Semrad

Did you know you can shine in every aspect of your life? We all can. First, we must break free from what is holding us back from realizing our fullest potential. Leaders empower, encourage, and inspire others to perform to their highest ability.[1] Yet, many are blind to what keeps them from greatness. Studies confirm self-limiting beliefs influence your daily actions and workplace performance, and prevent your career advancement.[2] Self-limiting beliefs are harmful and inaccurate thoughts about ourselves. I like to call these beliefs uninvited guests that

---

[1] Engstrom, T.W. (1976). *The Making of a Christian Leader: How to Develop Management and Human Resources Skills,* Grand Rapids, MI: Zondervan.
[2] Dickerson, A., & Taylor, M. A. (2000). Self-limiting behavior in women: Self-esteem and self-efficacy as predictors. *Group & Organization Management,* 25(2), 191-210. doi:10.1177/1059601100252006

restrain us from taking risks and maximizing our potential in business and our personal lives. Self-limiting beliefs feed and strengthen fear, greed, bitterness, shame, indifference, and loneliness. Unfortunately, leaders at all levels genuinely struggle to recognize their past left undealt will cripple their long-term effectiveness.[3]

H.E.R.A.C.T. is a framework anchored on research, real-life experiences, biblical principles, and the PERMA theory. The PERMA theory stands for positive emotions, engagement, positive relationships, meaning, and accomplishments. It is also known as the positive psychology theory to increase healthier and thriving human beings. While the PERMA theory continues to evolve, the theory has been around for the past decade. H.E.R.A.C.T. incorporates this proven theory throughout the framework and foresees similar successful outcomes.[4]

The H.E.R.A.C.T. framework combats head-on, self-limiting beliefs that get in the way of reaching our dreams. The H.E.R.A.C.T. framework challenges women to transform from the inside out and anchor their transformation in Jesus. The framework highlights the importance of healing, elevating your thoughts, and learning to respect and love yourself to achieve confidence and transformation.

Yes, despite our mistakes, we can re-write our narrative and experience a life-changing transformation. Your daily actions can move your transformation in the direction of your dreams. It starts with you and your commitment to ACTivating H.E.R.A.C.T.

---

[3] Blackaby, H. T., & Blackaby, R. (2011). *Spiritual leadership: Moving people on to God's agenda.* B&H Publishing Group.
[4] Coffey, J. K., Wray-lake, L., Mashek, D., & Branand, B. (2016). A multi-study examination of well-being theory in college and community samples. *Journal of Happiness Studies,* 17(1), 187-211.

in your life. If you want to activate the power you possess, unlock your potential, and fulfill your purpose, H.E.R.A.C.T. is for you. What is your strategy to arise and shine in every aspect of your life? Are you an individual who thinks of the glass as half-full, half-empty, or I'm going for more? Have you ever thought about going for more versus being complaisant? We must be willing to transform daily. Yet, after some time, many of us revert to old habits. Why do we revert to old habits? We often neglect to understand the root cause and only treat the symptom. We must seek to understand what is holding us back from continuously achieving our fullest potential. Leaders continually empower, encourage, and inspire others to perform to their highest ability.[5] Yet, many of us are blind to what keeps them from greatness. It is time to look in the mirror and sincerely answer this question, "Am I performing to the greatest of my abilities?"

A healthy mindset represents confidence, stability, and humility. On the other hand, an insecure leader often exhibits jealousy, fear, negativity, hate, anxiety, and impulsivity. In a society that values productivity over everything, it is all too easy for us to overlook our well-being and the impact on our professional and home life. Your decisions, past experiences, failures, and even accomplishments can weigh you down and keep you in a comfort zone, blocking you from becoming your best self. It is time to take control and prioritize your well-being or risk becoming a prisoner of your comfort and a death sentence to your dreams.

This book unveils that healing, elevation, and respect (H.E.R.) are essential ingredients for success. H.E.R.A.C.T. concentrates on the elements you can control regardless of your situation.

[5] Engstrom, T. W. (1976). *The Making of a Christian Leader: How to Develop Management and Human Resources Skills,* Grand Rapids, MI: Zondervan.

Through emotional healing, elevating your way of thinking, and loving yourself the way God loves, you will be able to defy your fears, activate your gifts, and achieve confidence and transformation (A.C.T.). When we invest in ourselves, we elevate our performance and those around us.

IN REAL LIFE: WE CAN CONQUER STRESS

One day, I woke up scholarly, accomplished, and financially stable with a high-profile executive job. My hard work had paid off. But what should have been a time of joy, fulfillment, and purpose was filled with void, torment, anger, and pain.

Trauma, life experiences, and harmful cultural messaging had made a home in my heart and mind. Achievements could no longer fill the void and quiet my pain. My body could no longer take the emotional, mental, and physical toll of long working hours to fulfill a dream that no longer brought me joy. Self-limiting beliefs had made me conform to ideas I had outgrown. The self-limiting beliefs of not feeling good enough, along with societal pressures, took center stage and attempted to stop me from achieving my fullest potential.

THE HARMFUL LIES WE BELIEVE

Self-limiting beliefs have haunted women for decades. Today's hyper-consumerist society influences us to pursue material things, status, titles, and careers. Only to later find we are miserable once we have achieved these things. Countless women lack peace and are filled with confusion because we have failed to heal and have compassion for ourselves and others. Many times, these harmful beliefs manifest as a result of trauma. Trauma has a way of hunting you even when you have forgotten about it. These limiting thoughts not faced head-on will destroy your career, relationships, health, and ultimately you.

Trauma relates to the absence of things we should have but never received, such as love and positive affirmations. Trauma also refers to what we may have received and did not ask for nor deserve, such as mental abuse, criticism, physical abuse, or abandonment. While there is a broad spectrum of the types of trauma a woman may experience, all trauma can be detrimental to well-being. Trauma impacts the way we live life and plants seeds of limiting beliefs along the way. These harmful seeds commence to bear fruit and cause stress, illness, and emotional fatigue.

Stress is a silent illness that causes havoc in your physical, mental, and emotional wellbeing. I experienced severe stress, and it was awful. I was on a two-year assignment outside of the United States. The position was a dream come true. Ensuring I exceeded expectations in a male-dominated environment pushed my body over the limit. I delivered against all odds, but my health paid the price. Stress slowly impacted my immune system, sleep, blood pressure, and mind. I woke up 25 pounds heavier, tired, and severely depressed one day. Stress is also a silent killer because it can lead to premature death. I remember opening my eyes in the morning and crying without understanding that my body was screaming for help. I finally saw a doctor. I found out the stress had shut down my metabolism and affected my thyroid. It wasn't too late for me, after carefully following the doctors' order, exercising, and putting my well-being first, I was able to leave all the medications behind and live a normal life.

Stress impacts the neocortex, also known as the thinking brain, affecting the limbic system known as the emotional brain. Not to worry; you do not need to have a degree in neuroscientist to connect the fact that the emotional brain enables distorted judgment; ask the parent of any teenager.[6] On March 14, 2017, the American Institute of Stress reported employers in the United States lost over $500 billion related to stress. Gallup reported over half of all Americans (55 percent) felt stressed daily in 2018. Almost half (45 percent) of people in the United States said they felt worried every day, and 22 percent reported chronic anger. In 2014 the American Psychological Center for Organizational Excellence reported 83 percent of health cases were due to employee depressions, stress, and anxiety (up 55 percent from 2012). It's worthwhile noting this data dates the pre-COVID-19 pandemic, making it even more critical for leaders to make well-being a priority.

SPIRITUAL CONNECTION

Uninvited guests can play with our minds and pivot our lives: daily dreams become lost, careers shatter, children are not born, relationships become more distant, and living seems impossible. Numerous opportunities pass us because these uninvited guests are now permanently making our minds their homes. Every woman has unique gifts to contribute to society, yet too many leave this world without birthing the treasure inside us. I believe your talent is the answer someone needs. However, limiting beliefs continue to shut the door to the fruits of the spirit. It is time you choose the fruits of the spirit which represent love, joy, peace, forgiveness, kindness, goodness, faithfulness, gentleness, and self-control.

---

[6] Morse, G. (2006). Decisions and desire. *Harvard Business Review*, 84(I), 42. Retrieved from: https://hbr.org/2006/01/decisions-and-desire

For a long time, I missed out on the fruits of the spirit. I invite you to taste the goodness, peace, and joy to see yourself how God sees you—as the apple of His eye. David tells us in Psalms 147:3 God heals the brokenhearted and binds up their wounds, but we must give it all to Him. No matter your situation, you can fulfill your purpose. The world puts limitations on God, but Paul clearly states in Philippians 4:13, you can do all things through Christ, for He is the one who sustains you.

YOUR TRANSFORMATION JOURNEY BEGINS NOW

H.E.R.A.C.T. is a life journey to well-being, not a destination. While many aspects impact your well-being, it starts with you. Throughout life, people will fail us. Your boss will let you down; your spouse may say the wrong thing; your close friends and family will betray you; your children will make mistakes; and let's face it, we will let ourselves down. Each time we fail to keep our promises to ourselves and others, we will let ourselves down. The reality is, the adversary uses the mind as a breeding ground for doubt. Every day we must work on H.E.R.A.C.T. to identify the root cause holding prisoner the fruits of the spirit. I invite you to elevate your way of thinking and view each day as a growth opportunity.

THE POWER OF OUR EMOTIONS

Our mental and emotional well-being faces a variety of headwinds each day. "It is literally neurobiologically impossible to build memories, engage complex thoughts, or make meaningful decisions without emotion."[7]

---

[7] Larby, K. *Mental Health and Wellbeing.* St Andrew's College. Retrieved from https://www.stac.school.nz/assets/Download-PDFs/General-PDFs/StAC-PERMA-V-in-the-classroom.pdf

Emotions impact our actions, and if we do not manage them, emotions will control our actions. The good news is, we have an exceptional capability to oversee and moderate our emotional reactions through reasoning and rationalizing.[8] Understanding and managing your feelings enables you to experience a healthier life. After all, emotions will influence what we enjoy and dislike. We need our emotions to love, experience joy, and pain. However, the right balance of positive emotions is required to build resilience and grow personally, professionally, and spiritually.[9]

Positive emotions are critical to our mental and emotional health. While difficult times are unavoidable, a healthy dose of positive thoughts will aid you in pushing through those obstacles. Positive thoughts can transform a problematic situation into a growth experience. Barbara L. Fredrickson, PhD, states negativity has its place; it can work as an essential warning in life. However, moving out of negative thoughts and emotions directly impact our performance. Overriding harmful negative thoughts is the most effective way to transform our feelings.

Jim Loehr, a world-renowned performance psychologist and co-founder of the Human Performance Institute, says, "Energy, not time, is the fundamental currency of high performance."[10] How we spend our physical, emotional, mental, and spiritual energy will continually determine our capacity to perform at our best.

---

[8] Hariri, Ahmad R.1; Bookheimer, Susan Y.1,2; Mazziotta, John C.1 Modulating emotional responses, NeuroReport: January 17, 2000 - Volume 11 - Issue 1 - p 43-48
[9] Seligman, M. (2011). PERMA-V: Our framework for well-being. Retrieved from https://www.stac.school.nz/why-stac/well-being-at-stac/perma-v/
[10] Loehr, J. & Schwartz, T. (2001). The making of a corporate athlete. *Harvard business review*, 79(1), 120-129.

Chapter 2:

HEALING

"Keep your vitality. A life without health is like a river without water."

~ Maxime Lagace

The H in H.E.R.A.C.T. stands for healing. Healing is essential to unlocking and sustaining your transformation. Healing enables your journey to see your greatness and activate your power. Generally, people think of healing in medical terms. In this book, healing refers to emotional and spiritual healing. Each person has unique life experiences that have left deep, open wounds. Wounds are painful to face, yet so necessary to heal. Recovery is personal; it is individual, and a standard medical protocol does not apply to emotional and spiritual healing. Healing feels like breathing after being underwater. It brings you life and enables you to bear fruit, and, most importantly, healing empowers you to enjoy the fruits of your labor.

Healing is vital to sustaining your best performance.

Have you ever seen a flowing river and all the growing life

around it? It is the same with leaders; people want to work with courageous, empathetic, confident, and humble leaders. Now, imagine a river without water—the vegetation dries out, and the animals that once quenched their thirst at the edge of the clear, peaceful running river move away for survival. Imagine a leader like the dry river. Many of us at some point represent the dry river, not because we lack the capacity to be a great leader, but because we struggle with recognizing our undealt past is crippling our long-term effectiveness. When we lead from an empty place, we appear egotistical, insecure, skeptical, and unreliable. I would not want to work for that type of leader. I would instead move as far as possible from them and seek growth in other places.[11]

While self-limiting beliefs surface differently for all of us, their history typically has deep and painful roots. Our past experiences can cause fear, greed, anger, envy, shame, guilt, lack of commitment, and much more, both at work and in our personal life. Many of us spend our lives living for the approval of others and envying those who receive the endorsement. While all these behaviors are highly harmful, envy and greed are incredibly dangerous to you and those around you. There is a very dark side to envy and greed, often leading to physical harm.

The unhealed wounds caused by your past will begin to rot and rob you of your life if not cared for appropriately.

FORGIVENESS FUELS YOUR POWER

Forgiveness plays a significant part in the healing process. It

[11] Blackaby, H. T., & Blackaby, R. (2011). *Spiritual leadership: Moving people on to God's agenda*. B&H Publishing Group.

is one of the most complex parts of the transformation journey. Yet, forgiveness is the ingredient often missing in the formula to activate our power. Forgiveness does not come easy, yet it is a virtue we must master if we want to activate our power. It is essential to note forgiveness does not mean we accept the other person's harm towards us as acceptable. It also does not mean disregarding, justifying, forgetting, or reconciling. It does mean you are no longer hanging on to someone else's sin. Sin separates us from God; it would be irrational to accept it. God is extremely serious about sin, to the point, He sacrificed His own Son for you and me.

Research, education, and therapy on forgiveness continue to gain academic and experimental attention. Studies validate forgiveness as a healing avenue for people experiencing deep emotional wounds, such as long-term emotional abuse and sexual abuse.[12] Unforgiveness and resentment compromise our emotional health and decision-making.[13] Nelson Mandela said it best: "Resentment is like drinking poison and then hoping it will kill your enemies." Studies on forgiveness have linked forgiving to improving self-esteem, depression, anxiety, and other negative thoughts.[14]

Forgiveness targets these emotional effects head on.[15] Additional studies confirm women, who exercise forgiveness due to emotional abuse, reclaim their purpose and live a more joyful life.

---

[12] Freedman, S. & Zarifkar, T. (2016). The psychology of interpersonal forgiveness and guidelines for forgiveness therapy: What therapists need to know to help their clients forgive. *Spirituality in Clinical Practice*, 3(1), 45–58.
[13] Reed, G.L., & Enright, R.D. (2006). The effects of forgiveness therapy on depression, anxiety, and posttraumatic stress for women after spousal emotional abuse. *Journal of Consulting and Clinical Psychology*, 74(5), 920–929.
[14] Freedman, S., & Zarifkar, T. (2016). The psychology of interpersonal forgiveness and guidelines for forgiveness therapy: What therapists need to know to help their clients forgive. *Spirituality in Clinical Practice*, 3(1), 45–58.
[15] Reed, G.L., & Enright, R.D. (2006). The effects of forgiveness therapy on depression, anxiety, and posttraumatic stress for women after spousal emotional abuse. *Journal of Consulting and Clinical Psychology*, 74(5), 920–929.

The forgiving theory pinpoints the root cause and uncovers injustice, anger, fear, or shame, to name a few. The forgiveness theory also involves forgiving and replacing resentment with goodwill. Many of us choose not to forgive and continue to expect something from the individual who caused us harm. Yet, expecting something from someone who cannot repay the damage is unrealistic and self-damaging. Only you can decide when you are ready to forgive. Remember, forgiveness does not mean reconciliation. The reality is some of us refuse to pardon people we interact with daily. Instead, we may choose to poison ourselves by fueling our hearts and minds with bitterness. King Solomon says in Proverbs 13:12, "Hope deferred makes the heart sick." Forgiveness releases the desire for a repayment that will never come.

Working on forgiveness is a must, or risk the resentment and limiting beliefs to continue to plague your mind, emotions, body, and soul.

It may feel easier not to forgive, blame the abuser for our failures, and credit our triumphs to our resilience. One major problem, the wound is still open. Forgiveness will demand a change in you. It will require moving past your fears and pushing past your limiting beliefs. Negative emotions manifest in all aspects of life when change occurs. Negative emotions toward change may manifest due to fear, loss of control, status, privilege, lack of trust, personal values, or simply aversion to change.[3] Negative emotions can convince you to boycott the change needed in your life to achieve the necessary transformation to perform at a higher level. If comfort is the ultimate objective, life changes become the biggest enemy.

SPIRITUAL CONNECTION

Scripture describes over 20 different emotions Jesus showed, including love, compassion, affection, anger, anguish, disappointment, peace, grief, sadness, and joy. Emotions are healthy. Nevertheless, sin has taken control of our feelings and distorted our actions. The Apostle John says in John 10:10 that the enemy comes to steal, kill, and destroy, but God comes to give life. God restores, cleanses, and transforms, but we must step out of our comfort zone. Nothing changes when you stay in your comfort zone. You must take the first step and invite God to be part of your healing. Ninety-seven percent of the women who answered the H.E.R.A.C.T. survey said their Top 3 enablers to recovery were their relationship with God, positive relationships, and forgiveness.

Most people have difficulty objectively understanding their broken areas and unintentionally build defense mechanisms. The beauty of having a relationship with God is He seeks to restore the broken emotions as part of our spiritual formation. After all, when we accept God, He lives in us. So, why not leverage Him to help us heal? God wants us to experience all the feelings healthily; after all, He created them. The stronger our relationship is with God, the more we grow spiritually. When we grow spiritually, our emotions and self-control also mature; it is a lifelong journey.[16] In Philippians 4:13, the Apostle Paul also tells us through Christ, we can do it all. When you have healthy emotional well-being, the fruits of the Holy Spirit are present in your life.

---

[16] McNicol, B., Willard, D., Thrall, B., Matthews, K., Fuller, P., Demarest, B., & Glerup, M. (2016). *The kingdom life: A practical theology of discipleship and spiritual formation.* Tyndale House Publishers, Inc.

PRACTICAL EXERCISE

Easier said than done. Where do we start? To address self-limiting beliefs, first, you must understand the root cause. To learn where the limiting beliefs stemmed from, you can ask yourself a series of questions. Pay attention to your emotions as you answer the questions and jot them down. Please do not ignore the feelings; it is vital to confront and recognize them as part of the healing process. It is normal to ignore the emotions, but ignoring them will only slow down your transformation. I invite you to be intentional about recognizing and acknowledging your feelings.

1. **Make a list.** List the people who have caused you pain, anger, bitterness. There is no time frame. Who did it? When? What did they do to you? How did it may you feel then? How does it make you feel now? Take your time; it is not easy to write down the name of someone who hurt you. The idea is to go back as far as you need to ensure you do not have unforgiveness in your heart. The list should include people who have neglected you and even taken advantage of you physically, financially, mentally, and emotionally.

   a. Is there something you should have received and never received, such as love, security, and affection?
   b. Have cultural messaging and conditioning caused self-limited beliefs to find a home in your heart and mind?
   c. What, who, or when triggers limiting beliefs in your life today?

d. How have the self-limiting beliefs affected your professional life, relationships, peace, and joy?
- How does it make you feel?

e. Our thoughts are powerful, but they are not always valid. Check yourself. Are the opinions that you think of you factual? Why or why not?

1. **Relinquish the bond of sin.** Forgiveness is a choice, and it is challenging. Do not be so hard yourself. Only when you decide to forgive genuinely will you begin your transformation. Yes, there will be flashbacks, but now you will be able to recognize the memories are not signs of things to come but a past that no longer dominates your present and future.

2. **Forgive one person at a time.** Name the abuser and, when you are ready and only when you are genuinely ready to forgive them, forgive them. You do not have to contact them or see them in person. Sometimes, for our safety, it is best not to see them in person. However, when you forgive genuinely, you can say out loud, "_____, I forgive you." Then pray for God to have mercy on them. It is ok if you do not get through the list. The goal is not to rush through the names but to genuinely take the time to forgive.

3. **Pray.** Pray for God to continue to heal your heart, mind, and soul. Ask for the Holy Spirit to intervene for you when you have no words to say. Ephesians 4:31 says, "Get rid of all bitterness, rage, and anger, brawling and slander, along with every form of malice. Be kind and compassionate, forgiving each other, just as Christ God forgave you."

YOU ARE NOT ALONE

Tarana Burke, the founder of the #MeToo movement, said, "The accused had not experienced the same type of trauma the survivors have and often do not want to apologize or take responsibility for their actions."[17] It's no wonder women have a hard time forgiving. New York Governor Andrew Cuomo made headlines in February 2021 when accused of creating a culture of sexual harassment within his administration. In a blog post by ex-staffer Lindsey Boylan, she echoes an all-too-familiar sentiment from women who are frequently asked, "Why didn't you speak out sooner?"

"There is a part of me that will never forgive myself for being a victim for so long, for trying to ignore behavior that I knew was wrong," Boyland wrote. "The governor exploited my weaknesses, my desire to do good work, and respect. I was made to believe this was the world I needed to survive in. It was all so normalized— articularly by Melissa DeRosa and other top women around him—that only now do I realize how insidious his abuse was."[18]

Because most women feel alone in traumatic experiences, speaking out about the trauma is incredibly challenging. We may feel shame and guilt for not standing up for ourselves or not knowing better. Shame is the overwhelming belief that our past becomes our identity. However, the truth is the world is broken, and shame lives freely among us. But if we aren't brave enough to share our stories, we will be unable to learn and heal from our experiences, and history will repeat itself.

---

[17] Carlsen, A., Salam, M., Cain Miller, C., Lu, D.,Ngu, A., Patel, J. & Wichter, Z. (2018). #MeToo brought down nearly 201 powerful men. Nearly half of their replacements are women. *The New York Times, https://www.nytimes.com/interactive/2018/10/23/us/metoo-replacements.html*

[18] Boylan, L. (2021). My story of working with Governor Cuomo. https://medium.com/@lindseyboylan4NY/my-story-of-working-with-governor-cuomo-e664d4814b4e

IN REAL LIFE: WE CAN FORGIVE

Jessica (names have been changed in the book) is an executive for a Fortune 500 company. Jessica shared the trauma she dealt with for years caused by a long-term, mentally and physically abusive husband. Although Jessica had been long divorced, she still carried bitterness into her new marriage. Jessica could not figure out why the anger controlled her. Single handedly, Jessica destroyed relationships at work and at home, and with the people she loved the most. The bitterness oozed out her every word, and impulsive negative actions followed. One day, someone asked her, "Why do you hate life so much?" Jessica felt guilty and thought long and hard about the question. She could not understand why she was so angry all the time.

Jessica had distanced herself from God and would only pray here and there. She no longer spent time in His presence. That night she came before God and prayed. To her surprise, God revealed to Jessica that she had only forgiven her ex-husband in words because she thought it was the right thing to do. She felt at church, that is what people wanted to hear. Secretly, Jessica had not forgiven him—deep down, Jessica was still expecting an apology and sometimes even contemplated vengeance. She recalls during the interview wishing him unhappiness and misery. Jessica realized something needed to change in her. She vaguely remembers the joyful person she used to be. Jessica invited God to remove bitterness from her heart. It was through prayer and strengthening her relationship with God she learned how to forgive. It took work for Jessica to truly forgive her ex-husband. She learned how to capture her thoughts and hold them captive to God's word. Today, Jessica is working on rebuilding the relationships she negatively affected due to the bitterness that once lived in her heart and unconsciously dictated her actions.

Scripture tells us in Ephesians 4:32 to forgive one another as Christ forgave us. As a reminder, forgiveness is something you do for yourself, not the person who wronged you. Matthew 26:28 also reminds us that Christ's death made possible the forgiveness of sins. We also find when God forgave us of our sins. He also cleansed us from all unrighteousness. The forgiveness theory shines the light on what scripture has guided us to do for centuries—forgive. When we forgive, it restores us.

Forgiveness enables positive emotions, positive relationships, spiritual growth, a sense of meaning, and empowerment.[19]

Working toward forgiveness always includes mourning and empathy for the person who caused you harm. It is critical to understand this because to forgive genuinely, you must be willing to let go of the thought the person who caused harm owes you. During forgiveness therapy, the grief work concentrates on effectively aiding the recovering woman to surrender resentment for the abuser. In the final phase of the forgiveness therapy, she discovers she is courageous because she decided to forgive.[20]

[10]Forgiving someone who deeply hurts us is uncomfortable because forgiving does not mean our mind and body will forget. It is a journey as the wounds heal into scars. Some days will remind you of painful memories of what has been, and other days you will have peace. The mention of a name can trigger physical and mental emotions. Some days are more tolerant

---

[19] Akhtar, S., Dolan, A., & Barlow, J. (2017). Understanding the relationship between state forgiveness and psychological wellbeing: A qualitative study. *Journal of Religion and Health,* 56(2), 450-463.
[20] Enright, R.D., & Fitzgibbons, R.P. (2000). *Helping clients forgive: An empirical guide for resolving anger and restoring hope.* Washington, DC: American Psychological Association.

than others. The good news is, we can choose our response. Forgiveness is a start to finding spiritual peace as you navigate the healing process. Scars will become a reminder of your courage and strength to have made it this far. Keep going; discover your power is limitless.

PRACTICAL EXERCISE

People cope with trauma and emotions differently. The reality is, people are dealing with grief, pain, anxiety, addiction, depression, and so many other things throughout the day. One exercise I often use in my conferences and find to be liberating is writing a letter of forgiveness to the person you are forgiving, whether you know their name or not. If you are forgiving more than one person, I recommend writing a letter to each individual. Suppose the person you need to forgive is yourself. I invite you to find a quiet place, invest the time, and write a letter to yourself. While the content and format are unique to you, it should include some of the following thoughts:

- **Letter opening.** Like a regular letter, address the letter to the person you are forgiving. Suppose you are writing to yourself, address the letter to your name.
- **Capture in the letter how your life was before the wrongdoing.** This part of the letter may sound something like this: "Before the incident, I was happy, whole, and secure." Take this opportunity to remember and write down who you were.
- **Describe how you felt during and after the offense.** In this section, I recommend you describe your feelings.

Write about the emotions you hide under your smile and speak to no one about. Please do not ignore your feelings; pay attention to them and write them down.

- **Define how the violation has affected you over time.** Write down self-limiting beliefs born of the incident or behaviors, fears, and life changes you have made due to the event.
- **Describe how you think the offender was feeling?** This one is personal to your situation and how you think they felt.
- **Show empathy for the person who committed the wrongdoing.** This part is critical because you may not be ready to forgive if you cannot find compassion, and that is OK. Sympathy does not excuse the person for wrongdoing. Come back to this step when you are ready. Once you are prepared to continue, this section of the letter may read something like: "You grew up in an abused home without love, and abuse is all you know."
- **Describe a positive that came out of the horrible experience.** This section may read something like: "I am grateful for the courage I found through this experience."
- **Declare your forgiveness intention and what you hope for you and the person that hurt you.** This part may read something like: "I choose to forgive you. I let go of my hate and the past holding me captive, and I look forward to the beauty of owning my power and fulfilling my purpose. I wish you peace and happiness."
- **Sign your name.** Wow! That was not easy. Take a moment to breathe and notice your emotions. Acknowledge them and take another deep breath. You are courageous. Hats off to you. You completed one of the most challenging exercises yet.

What you do with the letter is up to you. You can mail it, or you can shred it. The door to unleash your power is now open. Resilience is something only the survivors know. If you are reading this, you are a survivor. You are more resilient than you know; the power and courage you were born with are ready to reveal the best version of you.

IN REAL LIFE: TURNING GRIEF INTO HOPE

Mercy, another leader, shared she lost her 25-year-old child suddenly. Her grief consumed her, and peace was nowhere in sight. While losing a loved one is never easy, one of the biggest obstacles is the person's belief in their ability to survive the loss.[21] The person's thoughts and feelings and how they react to their emotions during significant life events determine how they cope. Many people struggle with feeling they could have done more. Others find gratitude for their time together. How they cope contributes to how they will manage life going forward. Studies show trauma can exaggerate the beliefs of personal responsibility.[22] The ability to control emotions is critical to how you spend your life.

Mercy told herself positive affirmations, entered therapy, and practiced gratitude. Yet, depression wanted to destroy her. Mercy stated she felt she had nowhere else to run and sought a relationship with Christ. Today, she credits her strength to find gratitude in her relationship with God. Through her daily talks with God, she finds the strength to endure her life's journey without her child. Mercy continues to practice affirmation and

---

[21] Kosminsky, P. (2017). CBT for grief: Clearing cognitive obstacles to healing from loss. *Journal of Rational - Emotive & Cognitive - Behavior Therapy*, 35(1), 26-37.
[22] Kosminsky, P. (2017). CBT for grief: Clearing cognitive obstacles to healing from loss. *Journal of Rational - Emotive & Cognitive - Behavior Therapy*, 35(1), 26-37.

gratitude; this time, her lens is from a spiritual level. While she misses her child daily, she has found peace, comfort, joy, and hope in Christ, knowing she will see her child again.

These testimonies are particularly traumatic. However, a constant barrage of more minor incidences of unwanted sexual harassment, microaggressions, mental abuse, and unwanted attention is enough to wear down a woman's confidence. Nevertheless, everyone's trauma is different.

Becky grew up in a rural area where she became desensitized to unwanted attention from men—the hug that lingered just a little too long, a hand placed just a little too low on her back, an unwanted gaze or comment. All of these things left her feeling uneasy, but if she were to protest, she was met with the words like, "You're too sensitive" or "I didn't mean anything by it." To help ourselves, our friends, and our daughters, it is imperative to normalize speaking out when something does not feel right. Holding others accountable for their words and actions is critical—only then can we hope for a better future.

SPIRITUAL CONNECTION

Shame is no stranger to God; in fact, shame was one of the first feelings experienced after the first sin in the Garden of Eden. When Eve and Adam sinned by eating from the forbidden tree, they tried to hide. We are no different today. Instead of seeking God, we rush to hide when we are hurt. We are afraid of what others would say, think, or do, and we choose to sit in shame.

Although the world says you should own your voice, we live in a society where standing up for what you believe in can result in being outcasted. If your opinion does not fit certain political narratives, you can count on being bullied into submission. In your journey of finding your voice, you must remember your timing starts when you are ready. Nevertheless, know that trauma and hurt are not your resting place; you are meant for more, and you know it. The world is waiting for you to arise and shine.

GRATITUDE INFUSES JOY

Gratitude also has proven to help heal and cope with traumatic life events. Practicing gratitude aids with the healing process and empowers us to impact the well-being of others.[23] Gratitude creates an encouraging emotional environment. When you operate in a state of gratitude, your mind and emotions shift—when we practice gratitude, we influence those around us. Leaders who express gratitude enable a positive work environment and enhance the well-being of their teams.[24] Practicing gratitude can be as practical as stating three things you are grateful for each day. It also can be as intense as journaling three things you are thankful for in your career, family, life, friendships, or finding the positive in the negative occurrences. However, if gratitude is not something that comes easily to you, I recommend starting small today.

PRACTICAL EXERCISE

Write three things you are grateful for today?

1. _____
2. _____
3. _____

---

[23] Jit, R., Sharma, C. S., & Kawatra, M. (2017). Healing a Broken Spirit: Role of Servant Leadership. Vikalpa: The Journal for Decision Makers, 42(2), 80−94.
[24] Jit, R., Sharma, C. S., & Kawatra, M. (2017). Healing a Broken Spirit: Role of Servant Leadership. Vikalpa: The Journal for Decision Makers, 42(2), 80−94.

FRIENDSHIPS HEAL

Google defines friendship as a person with whom one has a bond of mutual affection, typically exclusive of sexual or family relations. To be clear, we are not talking about your husband. I'm not talking about your associates or social media friends. In my opinion, social media should not classify people as your friends. To me, friendships are sacred, built over time, not overnight. I'm referring to the friends that when you call, even though time may have passed, your conversations pick up like it was yesterday. The friends that know your secrets and keep them under lock and key. These are the same friends that when you say you are going on vacation alone, they buy a ticket and show up on your flight. The friend who cries with you and celebrates your success. Friends are the ones that gently tell us the truth we do not want to hear and remind us of our worth. Friends are the ones who show up at our events without an invitation and support our dreams without hesitation. The friends that give you away at your wedding. The friends who come to your home and your heart aches when they leave. The same friend that prays for you, and you can count on all without expecting anything in return. I think you get the point. It is these types of friends that heal the soul. Different friendships may come and go through your life's different seasons; nevertheless, honor your friendships.

HEALTHY RELATIONSHIPS ARE ESSENTIAL

Establishing healthy relationships is a fundamental part of our lives. Healing restores emotional well-being, and relationships play a crucial role in the process.[25] David N. Elkins, PhD.,

---

[25] Elkins, D.N. (2015). *The human elements of psychotherapy: A nonmedical model of emotional healing.* Washington, DC: American Psychological Association.

professor emeritus of psychology, says supportive relationships are vital. Social support enables the brain's chemistry to work toward well-being. Elkins believes human beings can provide and receive emotional healing through positive relationships.[26] In a survey conducted of 35 executive women, 71 percent stated positive relationships contribute to overcoming self-limiting beliefs in the workplace and personal lives. Individuals with positive social ties experience happier lives.[27]

We spend our time surrounded by people who build, shape, and inspire our thinking and actions. Our minds are continually stimulated and influenced by the relationships we keep.[28] The brain needs stimulation to flourish; without it, the brain will die—constructive relationships promote positive emotions, neuroplasticity, and knowledge.[29] The Mayo Clinic published an article affirming inspiring friends influence your health. Positive relationships improve your sense of meaning, reduce stress, and positively impact your self-worth. Adults with strong social support reduce the risk of depression and high blood pressure. Most recent studies found individuals with positive relationships live longer.[30]

How would you rate your friendships? Most people under-leverage friendships as a powerful healing option for physical and mental well-being. Another study conducted on chronically

---

[26] Elkins, D.N. (2015). *The human elements of psychotherapy: A nonmedical model of emotional healing.* Washington, DC: American Psychological Association.

[27] Kihyun, L. (2016). Ethical Leadership and Followers' Taking Charge: Trust in, and identification with, Leader as Mediators. Social Behavior & Personality: An International Journal, 44(11), 1793-1802. doi:10.2224/sbp.2016.44.11.1793

[28] Cozolino, L. (2014). The Neuroscience of Human Relationships: Attachment and the Developing Social Brain (Norton Series on Interpersonal Neurobiology). United Kingdom: W.W. Norton.

[29] Ibid

[30] The health benefits of good friends. (2019, August 24). Retrieved January 08, 2021, from https://www.mayoclinic.org/healthy-lifestyle/adult-health/in-depth/friend-ships/art-20044860

depressed women found a significant improvement in their mental health when "prescribed" friends to visit and spend time with them. The findings were unbelievable. After the first year, the study found women with defined friends yielded the same success as traditional medication to manage depression and psychological interventions. The study also found that women with prescribed friends could find self-worth and live healthier lives.[31] In fact, oppression has thrived when the destruction of interpersonal solidarity occurs. "Nothing succeeds in breaking humans better than disrupting the bonds between them."[32] Guard the relationships that matter most to you by investing time in them. When you invest time in your relationships, you invest in your well-being.

There's an old saying: "It is lonely at the top." Unfortunately, women reach a point in their career when they can no longer raise concern to the leadership because no one looks like them. It is also challenging to find a support system below her because it is on her to set the emotional tone. It becomes even more important to find support outside of work during these times.

This love and support may come from a spouse, family member, friend, or daily prayer. Asking for help is a strength. You do not have to fight the darkness alone.

Relationships influence our lives more than we realize.[33]

---

[31] Sias, P. M., & Bartoo, H. (2007). Friendship, social support, and health. In *Low-cost approaches to promote physical and mental health* (pp. 455-472). Springer, New York, NY.
[32] Pépin, C. (2019). Self-Confidence: A Philosophy. United States: Other Press, LLC.
[33] Haden, J. (2017, October 21). A study of 300,000 people found living a longer, happier life isn't just about diet, exercise, or genetics. Retrieved January 02, 2021, from https://www.businessinsider.com/a-study-of-300000-people-reveals-the-keys-to-a-longer-happier-life-2017-10

PRACTICAL EXERCISE

- **Make a list** of friends or a friend from the past and present.
- **Take Action** Reach out to her today and let her know how much you appreciate her and your friendship. If you are having a hard time naming one person, it is time you activate mission friendship. Consider rekindling past positive friendships. If you cannot think of any past friendships, join an interest group, volunteer in the community, or join a faith community. I met my children's godmother in the faith community I joined when I moved to Texas. We started as church sisters, then became running partners, and now we are family; for life. Step out of your comfort zone and take the first step; the reward of having positive friendships is too high to leave it to chance.

SPIRITUAL CONNECTION

The Apostle Paul says in Thessalonians 5:11, "Comfort each other and edify one another." In the book of Ecclesiastes, Chapter 4, Solomon describes the value of a friend.

"Two are better than one,
"Because they have a good reward for their labor.
"For if they fall, one will lift his companion.
"But woe to him who is alone when he falls,
"For he has no one to help him up.
"Again, if two lie down together, they will keep warm;
"But how can one be warm alone?
"Though another may overpower one, two can withstand him.
"And a threefold cord is not quickly broken."[34]

---

[34] Ecc 4:9-12 (NRSV)

CHAPTER 3:

ELEVATE YOUR MINDSET

"The greatest limitations you will ever face will be those you place on yourself."

~ Denis Waitley

The answer lies in how we respond to life's positive and negative experiences. Hardship can build specific positive abilities in our character that could not develop without the negative experience. Your history does not make you a failure. Our ability to use our past as a stepping stone will determine our tomorrow. Still, self-limiting beliefs that go unchecked can cause serious harm to you, your future, your relationships, and those around you.

Do you believe you are designed for higher thinking? I do. Only humankind is created after its maker, and only humanity was made leader to rule over the earth. "Beliefs are the key to happiness and misery."[35] Did you know your mindset

---

[35] Dweck, C.S. (2008). *Mindset: The new psychology of success.* New York, NY: Random House Digital, Inc.

determines your professional and personal happiness? Studies show happy people are more productive than people with lower gratification.[36] These studies directly link and support the well-being of humans is vital to achieving their highest performance.

"This is how I am; since I can remember, I have always been like this!" It is easy to use your past, ethnic culture, and environment as excuses to stay in your comfort zone. I, too, have been guilty of using my past as an excuse for my actions. Jesus lived during a time when beliefs were deep-seated in the culture. Still, His calling was more significant than anyone could imagine. Chances are, your calling is more significant than you can imagine. The question is, will you choose to fulfill your purpose? Maybe your past is nothing you are proud of, or your future seems dark. The good news is you can change your narrative. You can choose to change your habits; you have the power to change the way you think and your beliefs about yourself. Sadly, many of us choose not to face our fears but instead give in to the limits we set for ourselves.

SPIRITUAL CONNECTION

Scripture tells us that the Israelites were enslaved in Egypt for 430 years. God appointed Moses to bring the Israelites out of slavery and take them to the promised land, a land flowing with milk and honey. However, the Israelites wanted to return to Egypt every time things got hard on the journey. They preferred returning to slavery, the very horrible treatment they escaped from, instead of elevating their mindset to freedom and possibilities in the promised land. Imagine this, the Israelites

---

[36] Oswald, A.J., Proto, E., & Sgroi, D. (2015). Happiness and productivity. *Journal of Labor Economics*, 33(4), 789-822.

lived in slavery, watching the Egyptians live free for years. They prayed for freedom, yet, they felt more comfortable in slavery. Too many of us are suffering in our comfort zone because the pain is too familiar. We are surviving but living without peace and joy.. We can no longer waste the powerful resource of our minds. We must take a chance, elevate our mindset, and create a life of peace and joy, a life we all have the right to live.

Headwinds will always be part of our lives; how we choose to handle them determines our growth. Scripture tells us the Israelites not only witnessed God's miracles, they lived them. Yet, their past oppression was blinding them from their freedom. When they saw the ocean in front of them, they saw defeat instead of hope. Fortunately for them, God is merciful, and He is in control. The Israelites had limited the power of God. Genesis 1:2 says, "The earth was formless and empty, and darkness covered the deep waters. And the Spirit of God was hovering over the surface of the waters." Having experienced God's numerous miracles, splitting the Red Sea in half should have been a no-brainer, yet once again, they were ready to throw in the towel.

Moses then "stretched out his hand over the Red Sea, and the Lord caused the sea to go back by a strong east wind all night, and made the sea into dry land, and the waters divided," the Israelites walked through the divided waters. Moses was in tune with God's voice. Are you? Are you hearing from God? Are you ignoring what He is telling you?

PRACTICAL EXERCISE

Think about your decision-making and ask yourself the following questions:

- What area is the uncertainty of tomorrow chaining you to the past? Explore your career, relationships, physical health, education, marriage, and everything in between.
- Are you letting your past dictate your future?
- What is stopping you from owning your narrative?

Elevating your mindset is another critical step of the H.E.R.A.C.T. If, as leaders, we do not elevate our perspective, we risk living in fear, muting our talents, and overemphasizing our weakness. What you believe, you hold onto, and while our thoughts may be powerful, they are not always right. When you do not know your potential, you can spend a lifetime exercising your weaknesses instead of soaring in your strength. Taking ownership of your mind is essential to elevating your mindset.

We receive over 11 million bits of information every day but can only consciously process 40 bits of information. An estimated 99 percent of the rest of the data is processed unconsciously. Our brains take shortcuts, that is how we are all wired, and most times, we subconsciously believe the untrue words we speak about ourselves. Our thoughts and behavior rise subconsciously in both positive and negative ways. We decide to confirm beliefs we already have, whether intentionally or unintentionally.

ASK YOURSELF

- Are you settling for the life you know of bondage and pain, or are you walking into the promised land?

Courageously owning your future starts with sharpening your focus and awareness of your mindset.

CULTURE INFLUENCES YOUR ACTIONS

The Eron Corporation achieved outstanding performance until the culture influenced the leaders and changed the future for the worse. Enron's downfall took place as a result of a fixed mindset culture. Organizational culture is hugely influential and incredibly powerful.[37] You may have heard the saying, "Culture eats strategy for breakfast." It is true—ask any leader who has tried to execute a strategy that clashes with its culture. Corporate culture represents what the company values and how the people within the organization think and act.[38]

Culture is the heart of the organization. If nourished with the right values, it is the organization's most potent secret weapon. Culture can enable an organization to reach its vision or cripple it. A fixed mindset culture will inhibit people from performing to their fullest potential. The Enron organization was known for recruiting the most talented and educated individuals. As a leader, "Who does not love great talent?"

There was only one problem, "Enron created a culture that worshiped talent and forced them into a fixed mindset."[39] The organization's fixed mindset culture created unintentional consequences. The high-potential superstar talent became risk-averse; they did not want to fail. Team failure was not an option to the leadership, and we know we grow through failure. We spend most of our adult life at work, and if you spend enough time in a fixed mindset culture, it will show its ugly head in your personal life choices.

---

[37] Schneider, W.E. (2000). Why good management ideas fail. *Strategy & Leadership,* 28(1), 24-29.

[38] Yafang, T. (2011). Relationship between Organizational Culture, Leadership Behavior and Job Satisfaction. *BMC Health Services Research, 11*(1), 98-106.

[39] Dweck, C.S. (2008). *Mindset: The new psychology of success.* New York, NY: Random House Digital, Inc.

ASK YOURSELF

- Are you afraid to fail?
- Are you leaving growth opportunities on the table because the culture you grew up in demands excellence?

YOUR MINDSET DETERMINES YOUR FUTURE

Based on her 20-plus years of research, Standford University psychologist and American Psychological Association award-winner Carol Dweck found our thoughts powerfully influence our lives."[40] A fixed mindset assumes that our character, acumen, and creative ability are static givens and do not need fixing."[41] On the contrary, a growth mindset flourishes on challenges and sees setbacks as a learning experience to grow and build new capabilities. Our mindset will limit or enable our professional and personal growth. The difference between the two perspectives determines who you become. It is mind-blowing the power our mind possesses. Our mind has the power to control our future. A growth mindset pushes you beyond the comfort zone and confirms all can transform and grow.[42]

On the other hand, a fixed mindset expects all good things to happen without effort. People with a fixed mindset believe love magically occurs in a relationship, like fairy tales or romantic comedies. I hate to break it to you, but there is no such thing as a fairy tale. All relationships need work. A professional relationship and a personal relationship need work. The fixed mindset will surface evidence to judge individuals and prove why others are

---

[40] Dweck, C. S. (2008). *Mindset: The new psychology of success.* New York, NY: Random House Digital, Inc.
[41] Dweck, C. S. (2008). *Mindset: The new psychology of success.* New York, NY: Random House Digital, Inc.
[42] Popova, M. (2014). Fixed vs. Growth: The two basic mindsets that shape our lives. *Brain Pickings.*

responsible for the relationship's failure. A growth mindset sees conflict as an opportunity for learning how to improve versus judge. A growth mindset seeks input to process knowledge and productive action.[43] Dr. Dweck believes that the growth mindset's trademark is your desire to challenge yourself even when it seems impossible.[44]

The silver lining is most of the best things in life are hard to achieve. If they weren't, everyone would do them. Although the longer you live with a fixed mindset, the more difficult it is to learn a growth mindset perspective. The good news is that it is possible to change your mindset. The first thing you need to do is be aware of your thoughts. A fixed mindset will tell you, "You are not worthy" or "You are not qualified." Do not take the bait. A growth mindset will never diminish your potential.

To begin transforming your mind, listen to your thoughts; you must use your imagination to write down your vision, goals, and action plan for growth. To inspire a growth mindset in others, you must listen, give credit, encourage, and nurture the possibilities. With each challenge you face, think of the growth opportunities. The world does not owe you anything, but you owe it to yourself to bring the best version of yourself to life. Stop doubting yourself, and let me repeat this. Yes, you can achieve a growth mindset. A growth mindset elevates your perspective and will help you thrive in every aspect of your life. Our minds are powerful, and the enemy seeks to control them. Take back your mind and own and activate the power that lives within you. It must stay dormant no more!

---

[43] Popova, M. (2014). Fixed vs. Growth: The two basic mindsets that shape our lives. *Brain Pickings*.
[44] Dweck, C.S. (2008). *Mindset: The new psychology of success*. New York, NY: Random House Digital, Inc.

IN REAL LIFE: A RESILIENT MINDSET GETS YOU
OVER THE FINISH LINE

People with a growth mindset look at their failures and challenges in the face and move forward while having the faith that they will thrive.[45] Tom Whittaker became the first disabled person to summit Mount Everest, the highest mountain in the world. Years before climbing Mount Everest, Whittaker had lost his foot due to a car accident and walked with a prosthetic foot. Instead of limiting himself, he set his mind to climb Mount Everest. It is a dangerous mountain to climb with a high fatality rate. The mountain is so formidable that most of the deceased climber's bodies remain in the mountain. The only year with unknown deaths at Mount Everest was in 1977.

Nonetheless, Whittaker was determined to reach the summit. On his third attempt, through the pain, viral infections, and freezing temperatures, he summited Mount Everest on May 27, 1998. Whittaker clearly had a growth mindset. Every time he failed to summit, he learned to come back stronger. Whittaker became a role model and inspiration to many, including others with disabilities.

In 2001 Erik Wihenmayer became the first blind man to summit Mount Everest. Mark Inglis became the first double amputee to climb Mount Everest in 2006. Arunima Sinha was thrown off a moving train by muggers and lost a leg when the train ran over her leg. She became the first female amputee to summit Mount Everest in 2011. The list goes on. In 2015, Nepal announced it would not give permits to people with significant disabilities because of the extreme dangers; 19 people died that year. I'm

[45] Dweck, C.S. (2008). *Mindset: The new psychology of success.* New York, NY: Random House Digital, Inc.

not asking you to put your life on the line, but I do want to emphasize your mindset determines how far you go. Go ahead, apply for the promotion, start a business, write a book, ask for a raise, answer that call, start the family you have been putting on hold, get the puppy, and please go on vacation!

Your mindset and determination will enable you to succeed against all odds.

SPIRITUAL CONNECTION

Goliath, a giant and known champion from the Philistine army, challenged the Israelite army to single-man combat. The winner of the fight would have the opposing army as their servants. Every Israelite warrior was terrified, including their leader, King Saul. David saw Goliath as an opportunity. David was experienced fighting animals in the wild and had killed a bear and lion while protecting his herd of sheep. David believed in the power God had placed in him, and that was all the confidence he needed to take down the giant. "You come to me with a sword, with a spear, and with a javelin. But I come to you in the name of the Lord of hosts," said David. David prevailed over the Philistine with one stone; he struck the Philistine and killed him. David leveraged his talents and used his weapon of choice, a slingshot. He did not go after Goliath with a sword. David used the skills God had placed in him and defeated the giant. He believed in the power of God within him. He was determined to win and set the army free of fear. David took action and leveraged his skills with the slingshot to bring victory to Israel. David did not allow the people around him to hold him back from leveraging his strengths to win the battle. We all have unique gifts; stop comparing your talents to hers. We need your gifts. Are you leveraging your talents, or do you believe they are not good enough to claim your victory?

Betrayal, turmoil, and prison could not stop Joseph from becoming one of Egypt's most powerful leaders. Joseph was a happy young child extremely loved by his parents until his brothers betrayed him. Joseph's brothers became jealous of him and sold him to traders. The joy and love he knew were now only a memory; slavery and turmoil ruled his present. However, Joseph's faithfulness to God enabled him to have a growth mindset. Joseph leveraged his strengths and eventually became a steward to Potiphar. When you rise, people will want to see you fall. Potiphar's wife framed Joseph and accused him of a crime he did not commit. Once again, the joy he knew came to an end.

Life had not been fair to Joseph, but that did not stop him from using his talent. Joseph's loyalty to God was unbreachable. He did not let his environment and circumstances prevent him from strengthening and using his abilities. Joseph thrived even in prison. Joseph became the right-hand man to the warden in a short time and was assigned over all the prisoners. Despite all the unfavorable circumstances, Joseph continued his loyalty to God and was grateful for his life.

Fast forward, Pharaoh made Joseph governor of Egypt and the second highest in command after Pharaoh. Little did he ever imagine that he would go from the prisoners' responsibility to the responsibility of a whole nation.

What you may be going through now may be preparing you for the most significant breakthrough in your life. Exercise a growth mindset and stay faithful.

When famine came over the land, Joseph's brothers came looking for food—the same brothers who betrayed him. The same ones who stole his childhood and moments with his father and now diseased mother had come to Egypt looking for food. Joseph did what many struggle to do—he forgave his brothers. Joseph experienced difficult times and achieved more than many of Egypt's sons. Little did Joseph know that he could save his father and brothers from the famine one day because of his powerful position. Life will have mountains and valleys. Although we may not understand how the pain will benefit the future, our mindset will determine if we keep our eye on the vision or sacrifice our position.

UNDERSTANDING YOUR STRENGTHS

Understanding your strengths starts with self-analysis. Hundreds of self-assessment tools are accessible through the internet. Studies also continue to surface an extensive list of leadership traits. American business executive and leadership author Harry Kramer calls out four essential principles: self-reflection, a balanced outlook, confidence, and sincere humility.[46] Peter Northhouse, professor of communication at Western Michigan University, adds intelligence, confidence, willpower, integrity, and sociability. The lists go on and on, yet no one list is the picture-perfect recipe for a flawless leader.[47] One leadership trait gaining more energy is self-awareness.[48]

---

[46] Kraemer, H.M. (2011) *From Values to Action: The Four Principles of Values-Based Leadership.* San Francisco, CA: Jossey-Bass.

[47] Northhouse, P.J. (2016). *Leadership Theory and Practice, 7th edition,* Oaks, CA: Sage Publications, Inc.

[48] Bratton, V.K., Dodd, N.G., & Brown, F. W. (2011). The impact of emotional intelligence on the accuracy of self-awareness and leadership performance. *Leadership & Organization Development Journal,* 32(2), 127-149.

Making a conscious effort to discover more about yourself each day will make a long-term impact on the way you view yourself.

SPIRITUAL CONNECTION

In the book of John 4:5, Jesus encounters a Samaritan woman fetching water from a well. When Jesus asked her for a drink, her anguish blinded her, and she did not recognize the living water, Jesus Christ. Her self-limiting beliefs allowed her only to see her failures and the negativity around her. Instead, she asked why he would ask her, a Samaritan woman. The Samaritan woman had lived with five different husbands, and the man she was currently involved with was not her husband. Society categorized her as a woman of no worth, and she believed the lie.

God sees beyond what people see. He saw her worth. However, her past kept her from seeing the truth of her potential. The moment she saw Jesus and not her past, she experienced truth. "Many of the Samaritans in that city believed in Him because of the word of the woman." She made a significant difference that day.

ASK YOURSELF

- Is your past blinding you from the blessings that are right in front of you?
- Have you passed on an opportunity, a relationship, a promotion, or your dreams?

Your past choices do not define you. It is time to remove the veil that has kept you from seeing the truth; you are worth it, enough, victorious, intelligent, capable, loved, beautiful, and powerful.

SELF-AWARENESS

Understanding yourself is essential to growing as an individual and as a leader to empower yourself and those around you.[49] In a small start-up business with limited resources in large corporate America, knowing your strengths and weaknesses can make a difference in the marketplace and the industry. Self-awareness also means understanding why certain things are strengths and why others are weaknesses. Understanding what shaped you to be who you are today will be essential. It will mean digging deeper and understanding how your strengths and weaknesses impact those around you. It also means investing in your strengths while surrounding yourself with those who are experts in the areas where you're weak. After all, people who leverage their strengths report to be happier, more engaged, and walking in the purpose.

Today self-awareness also means knowing your cultural biases and how culture has shaped your identity.[50] Do you know the doors your identity opens and close? There are doors that open and close simply because of your identity. As a Latina and a mother, I have found closed doors in certain places because of my identity. As an executive, I have found doors that are open.

As an executive, there are doors that open. Knowing your identity will allow you to strategically leverage your power to hold the door open for others or seek the support of those that have access to an open door. Imagine the impact you can have in your life and those around you if you invest time in self-discovery. Lack of self-awareness will negatively impact your growth and

---

[49] Caldwell, C., & Hayes, L.A. (2016). Self-efficacy and self-awareness: moral insights to increased leader effectiveness. *Journal of Management Development.*

[50] Van Velsor, E.V., McCauley, C.D., & Ruderman, M.N. (Eds.), 2010. *The Center for Creative Leadership Handbook of Leadership Development,* (3rd Ed.) San Francisco, CA. Jossey-Bass.

the growth of those you lead.[51] Whatever we put our mind, time, and effort into becomes our reality. The more self-aware leaders are of both their identities and understanding their strengths and weaknesses, the easier it is for them to develop genuine and successful relationships."[52] Cam Caldwell, PhD, author and professor at the University of Illinois at Springfield, says, "Self-awareness is an effort. It is a conscious effort to invest in understanding who we are, our universal rules that (we) apply in life, and our commitment to the future."[53]

Nonetheless, successful leadership also begins with humility.[54] It takes humility, intentionality, and hard work to see the truth. Humility is crucial in the journey to discover and love who we are and who we can become.[55] Elevating our minds also requires being intentional about the language we use. Our words also can create our reality. Proverbs 18:21 reminds us the tongue has the power of life and death. Pay attention to your words. Are you quick to speak about your faults, weaknesses, failures, opportunities, and the reasons why things cannot be done? Or do you rise and speak life to your darkness? The world will continuously try to tear you down. You must maintain and nourish your self-esteem and self-confidence by speaking life. When you rise out of bed, make it a habit to speak life into your life.

---

[51] Clark, J. (2015) *The Five Principles of Global Leadership How To Manage the Complexities of Global Leadership*. Bloomington, IN: WestBow Press.

[52] Caldwell, C. (2009). Identity, self-awareness, and self-deception: Ethical implications for leaders and organizations: JBE. *Journal of Business Ethics*, 90, 393-406. doi:http://dx.doi.org.ezproxy.regent.edu:2048/10.1007/s10551-010-0424-2

[53] / Gallo, S., Editor Training Industry, Partners, V., & Gehrke, J. (2020, July 27). The Importance of Self-awareness in Leadership. Retrieved from https://trainingindustry.com/articles/leadership/the-importance-of-self-awareness-in-leadership/

[54] Engstrom, T.W. (1976). *The Making of a Christian Leader: How to Develop Management and Human Resources Skills*, Grand Rapids, MI: Zondervan.

[55] Gallo, S., Editor Training Industry, Partners, V., & Gehrke, J. (2020, July 27). The Importance of Self-awareness in Leadership. Retrieved from https://trainingindustry.com/articles/leadership/the-importance-of-self-awareness-in-leadership/

SPIRITUAL CONNECTION

In James 3, we are warned about the taming of the tongue. When we put bits into horses' mouths to make them obey us, we can turn the whole animal. Or take ships as an example. Although they are enormous and driven by strong winds, they are steered by a small rudder wherever the pilot wants to go. Likewise, the tongue is a small part of the body, making great boasts. Consider how a great forest is set on fire by a tiny spark. Our language can act as that destructive forest fire. It can become a world of evil among the parts of the body. The tongue is capable of corrupting our whole body, sentencing the entire course of our life to death. Our tongue can be release poison or life; you choose how you want to use this powerful weapon you possess. I invite you to speak life.

Scriptures say that we praise our Lord and Father with the tongue, and with it, we curse our neighbor. Out of the same mouth come praise and cursing. My brothers and sisters, this should not be. Can both fresh water and saltwater flow from the same spring? My brothers and sisters, can a fig tree bear olives or a grapevine bear figs? Neither can a salt spring produce fresh water.

PRACTICAL EXERCISE

Speak life to yourself. Let's practice. How you speak matters, and the harsh words others say to you can cause long-term damage. Being diligent in refusing any harmful, dishonest words to come out of your mouth will be critical. The same way your thoughts have power, so do the words you speak. Go ahead, take control.

- What is the one negative thing you believe about yourself?
    - For me, it was that I could never be a successful executive, a good mother, and a happy wife.
- What words do you continue to hear in your head?
    - For me, it was you are not good enough.
- What is the one thing you have been struggling with, such as losing weight, finishing school, meeting your husband, relationships, advancing your career, or self-love?
    - For me, it was discipline.

Affirmations elevate the thoughts we have of ourselves and offer encouragement.[56] I invite you to resist the urge to reject beautiful words said to you. It may feel uncomfortable initially, but start by responding, "Thank you for your kind words." Then, stop there. Negative thoughts will always be ready to attack, and they will reach your subconscious. The secret weapon is to remind yourself of the truth. Scripture has countless facts for everyday life. Some of my favorites include:

- You are fearfully and wonderfully made in God's eyes. (Psalm 139:14)
- You are complete in God's eyes. (Colossians 2:10)
- You are loved in God's eyes. (Jeremiah 31:3)
- You are worth delighting in. (Zephaniah 3:17)
- You are forgiven and redeemed in God's eyes. (Ephesians 1:7)
- You are anointed and have a purpose in God's eyes. (Isaiah 61:1)

---

[56] Van Velsor, E.V., McCauley, C.D., & Ruderman, M.N. (Eds.), 2010. *The Center for Creative Leadership Handbook of Leadership Development,* (3rd Ed.) San Francisco, CA. Jossey-Bass.

- You are beautiful in God's eyes. (Psalm 45:11)
- You are more than a conqueror in God's eyes. (Romans 8:37)
- You are chosen, holy, and dearly loved in God's eyes. (Colossians 3:12)
- You are God's handiwork. (Ephesians 2:10)
- You are set free in God's eyes. (Galatians 5:1)
- You are a new creation in God's eyes. (2 Corinthians 5:17)

Your words are a powerful secret weapon. Exercise your authority wisely.

IMAGINATION

"Your mind is like a parachute; it only works if it's open." - **Frank Zappa**

Individuals are not one-dimensional; we are unique and, therefore, beautifully complicated. Our experiences, religion, culture, ethnicity, gender, social status, and many other areas make us unique. As leaders, discovering and implementing innovative solutions in our organizations is essential for the business's growth. Yet, we neglect to think creatively and elevate our way of thinking regarding our lives. There are hundreds of tools organizations use to innovate. We know the tools work. The question is, why are we not leveraging these tools for our personal growth?

Brainstorming is one of those tools. In an organization, brainstorming works best when people of different backgrounds and experiences capture innovative ideas to solve a specific problem [57] From a personal development perspective, brainstorming allows you to identify areas holding you back from becoming your best self. Accepting criticism is not easy, but it is essential for our growth. It is beneficial to include trustworthy people who know you well during your brainstorming process. Inviting others into the brainstorming session will be necessary to identify any blind spots. Listening to others' perceptions enables your mind to see yourself differently. Warning: Please make sure to have an open mind when listening to others. Not all feedback is worthy of action, but all input should be analyzed with an open mind.

PRACTICAL EXERCISE

- Invest time today in understanding what is holding you back from realizing your dreams. Take a moment and write down every possible relationship, emotion, experience, and current situation that comes to mind that you feel may be holding you back. Write down even those thoughts that popped in your mind, even if you think they have no merit.
- What is missing in your life?
- Do you have peace with where you are in life?
- Do you manipulate your relationships?
- Do you attract the same toxic relationships, only different people, to your life?
- How do you describe your relationships?
- Do you have big dreams but procrastinate about putting them into motion?

---

[57] Michalko, M. (2006). *Thinkertoys a handbook of creative-thinking design.* Berkeley: Toronto. Ten Speed Press. PP.311.

- What is the one thing you can do differently today to address the questions above?

I know it is difficult to pick one thing, but trust me picking more than one thing will be unrealistic. It is the discipline for me. However, practicing and being disciplined in all I do has changed all aspects of my life.

Possibly you know what is missing in your life but struggle with how to solve it. Our minds cannot expand while there is an existing gap between who you are and the imagination of how far you can go. You must begin by removing the limits you have set on yourself.

Understanding yourself brings you one step closer to elevating your mindset.

SPIRITUAL CONNECTION

The Apostle Peter reminds us in 1 Peter 4:10 your gifts are meant to serve one another; do not neglect your gifts. "Let your light so shine that they may see your good works and glorify your Father in heaven."

God gave us one of the greatest gifts as human beings—our imagination. Awaken the precious and powerful gift of your imagination; capitalize on your creativity. While people put great focus on Intelligent Quotient and Emotional Quotient, the human imagination supersedes them. In an organization, imagination is priceless because creativity influences the next billion-dollar idea. In the workplace, imagination starts with a prototype. Prototypes are altered, changed, and tweaked multiple times until the perfect product is born. How does

a prototype compare to a human being? I'm glad you asked
Our lives are a work in progress; we continuously work on a
better version of ourselves the same way organizations work
on a better version of their product. Take a look at the iPhone.
Each year it gets better. Sometimes they are significant changes;
other times, small changes. To realize the best version of you,
you must remove the barriers in your imagination.

Gary Hamel, a management expert, said, "Not operational
excellence, technology breakthroughs, or new business models,
but innovation fuels long-term growth."[58] Everyone has creativity
and innovation, but unfortunately, we limit our imagination and
weaken our creation. As leaders in a corporation, the community,
or our homes, we are responsible for enabling a culture that
rewards failure, invests in learning, and empowers creativity.

SPIRITUAL CONNECTION

Expert Gary Oster says, "God freely opens opportunities to
engage in heaven-guided innovation to every person."[59] Oster
also challenges us to know who we are in Christ. Matthew says
in Matthew 6:33 to "Seek first the kingdom of God and His
righteousness." Sadly, too many of us get stuck on religion
and lack an intimate relationship with Christ. When we practice
religion, we set boundaries for Christ. We leave Him in the four
walls of the church and limit his dominion. We make a mistake
when we exclude God as a partner to turn to when dealing with
personal and business decisions. Resisting the temptation to limit
God and your imagination will help you step up to a new level.

---

[58] Hamel, G., & Breen, B. (2007). *The future of management.* Boston, Mass: Harvard Business School Press.
[59] Oster, G. (2011) *The Light Prize Perspectives on Christian Innovation.* Virginia Beach, VA: Positive Signs Media.

Continuous learning is another way to keep you from sitting on the complacent couch too long. Knowledge management will feed your creativity. What we continually feed our minds will bear fruit. If Joseph had allowed fear, defeat, and failure to rule his future, his circumstances would have defeated him. Instead, his growth mindset and faithfulness to God outshined the darkness.

Evaluating your network is another vital step. Do you surround yourself with innovators, people who inspire you, people who take risks? Or do you surround yourself with people who settle for the status quo or people who only look like you and you only feel comfortable around? Have you outgrown your current network? Find people who excel in creativity. Find people different than you. You are not looking to become the best innovator overnight, but yes, you are looking to jumpstart your imagination. You can jumpstart your creativity by learning from others. Our mind is limitless, and we must elevate our thoughts and intentionally renew the mind.

Surrounding yourself with people who shut down your creativity is a risk you should not take. Your ability to think limitlessly about your potential is a transferable skill into your professional life. Leaders understand the organization must continuously innovate to compete in the marketplace. To power your team with an innovative mindset, leaders must remove innovation antibodies that interfere with the organization's growth, even if it means allowing others to lead the project. It takes the humility of a great leader to be self-aware of their strengths and let others shine. It takes humility to see the bigger picture. Remember, you can learn from other creative people around you—enable them to shine.

ASK YOURSELF

- Visualize and ask yourself: "Wat if the solution to living my best life lies in what is missing?"

Countless people only experience a portion of their potential because they fail to elevate their mindset. Our dreams have become a thing of the past because fear paralyzes our imagination. Imagine if your history and your failures hold the key to your transformation. Remember, your mindset determines the meaning of failure. Put aside all things in the way of your dreams and imagine your life without limits—the possibilities.

SPIRITUAL CONNECTION

You must disturb your thinking by imagining beyond your comfort zone to elevate your perspective. Comfort zones create conformity, and you were not born to idle; you were born to shine. King Solomon says in Proverbs 31:27, "She watches over the ways of her household, and does not eat the bread of idleness." Transformation begins in the uncomfortable zone. The Apostle Paul urges us in Romans 12:12 to not be conformed by this world but to transform by renewing the mind. We cannot elevate our mindset if we continue to feed on the limitations of the flesh. To receive the wisdom and creativity only He can give, one must connect to the power source, Jesus Christ. Christ is the most significant innovator of all time.

The way you feel is the way you will lead. As leaders, we have a significant responsibility to inspire and elevate the mindset of others. To avoid planting limiting beliefs on others, we must remain flexible to new ways and open to learning. We must also resist the temptation to shut down someone else's idea without words of encouragement. These unintentional consequences impact long-term productivity and long-term personal well-being. You do not want an employee to shut down and give up on what could be the next business breakthrough.

LET YOUR VALUES BE YOUR NORTH STAR

Understanding our values, what is true, emotions, dreams, strengths, and fears equips us to step out of our comfort zones. As leaders, it is crucial to understand your values. Values are what you stand for in public and private, regardless of the consequences. Your actions impact people—be mindful of the shadow you cast.[60] A leader's values reflect what is important to them. Knowing, understanding, and acting on your values will shape your virtue and, ultimately, your character. Our relationship with Christ determines how we view ourselves and the world. The question is, "Are you spending time living your value, or the values the public influences on you?"

Your values will impact your moral and non-ethical actions and bring to light your personality as a leader.[61] Lamentably, many of us believe our actions are ethical. However, studies show numerous daily activities are dishonest and move us further away from modeling ethical behavior.[62] The good news is there is an opportunity to shape our character each day. We can develop our character by continuously correcting actions that may lead us toward destruction.[63] Breaking old habits is not easy but

[60] Kerns, C.D. (2014). Strengthening Values Centered Leadership; What, Why and How? Graziado Business Review. 7(2).
[61] Fedler, K.D. (2006). *Exploring Christian Ethics Biblical Foundations for Morality.* John Knox Press. Louisville, KY.
[62] Badaracco, J.L. (1997). *Defining Moments, When Managers Must Choose Between Right and Right.* Boston, MA: Harvard Business Review Press.
[63] Maxwell, J.C. (1999). The 21 Indispensable Qualities of a Leader, Becoming the Person Others Will Want to Follow. Nashville, TN. Thomas Nelson, Inc.

can be done by intentionally fixing the behavior. One way to intentionally develop your character is to work on one thing that impacts all aspects of your life. Being disciplined in the workplace and at home will keep you focused and intentional about all you do. Being disciplined is as simple as asking yourself questions, such as "Would a disciplined person be multitasking while listening to a loved one? Would a disciplined person over-eat? Would a disciplined person leave for tomorrow what they can do today?" "Would a disciplined person not prepare for the future?"

A leader's character is critical. It is more than a title; the way you engage matters because the shadow you cast impacts the people around you. Your behavior influences the level of trust and impact you have with others. Shaping your character takes time, but it forces you to engage and, most importantly, invest in a better version of yourself. Modeling the way is a leadership competency we must all take extremely seriously and keep top of mind.[64]

Integrity also plays a critical role in our actions and sustaining genuine long-term relationships at home and in the marketplace. Inauthentic leadership does not inspire trusting relationships. Honesty and integrity undoubtedly play a crucial role in inspiring the best in others. Studies show leaders who encourage and inspire their teams to realize their highest performance typically display genuine honesty and integrity.[65] High-performing leaders focus on building trusting relationships and enabling a culture of collaboration. All relationships strengthen with trust.

[64] Kouzes, J.M., & Posner, B.Z. (2007). *The leadership Challenge*, 6th edition, San Francisco, CA: Jossey-Bass.
[65] Engstrom, T.W. (1976). *The Making of a Christian Leader: How to Develop Management and Human Resources Skills*, Grand Rapids, MI: Zondervan.

We determine if we want to work for a leader in the workplace based on their actions.[66] Outside of work, it is the same. We do not want to associate with people who are not trustworthy. Integrity, honesty, gratitude, compassion, and humility are critical elements of effective leadership linked to spiritual leaders. One of the most inspiring spiritual behaviors is demonstrating love and respect for others. "Treating others fair is a natural consequence of viewing them with respect. Justice and fairness are values important to most spiritual paths, since mistreating others indicate a lack of respect, compassion, and integrity."[67]

Unfortunately, we all suffer from the toxic nature of sin. Sinful nature manifests when we make decisions against God's will. Sometimes we invite corruption into our lives by our actions, words, and toxic relationships we keep. There are other times when sin is forced upon us by another. Sin often takes us into a deep cave of isolation. We place too much of our precious time fighting the wrong battles. When we understand our worth before God, we will value ourselves.

Integrity plays an integral part in all you do. We must exhibit honesty and integrity to achieve greatness.

An honorable person does not need a reminder to execute with excellence; they naturally act ethically.[68] Sadly, during times of uncertainty and pressure, people risk their integrity.[69]

---

[66] Gilstrap, J. B., & Collins, B.J. (2012). The importance of being trustworthy: Trust as a mediator of the relationship between leader behaviors and employee job satisfaction. Journal of Leadership & Organizational Studies, 19(2), 152-163. doi:10.1177/1548051811431827.

[67] Reave, L. (2005). Spiritual values and practices related to leadership effectiveness. *The Leadership Quarterly*, 16(5), 655-687. doi:10.1016/j.leaqua.2005.07.003.

[68] Fedler, K.D. (2006). *Exploring Christian Ethics Biblical Foundations for Morality.* John Knox Press. Louisville, KY.

[69] Bischoff, S. J., DeTienne, K.B., & Quick, B. (1999). Effects of ethics stress on employee burnout and fatigue: An empirical investigation. *Journal of Health and Human Services Administration*, 21(4), 512-532.

There is no shortage of examples of people like you and me who sacrificed their integrity and lost it all. You can avoid tempting to sacrifice your integrity by surrounding yourself with trusted friends and advisors who will counsel you when observing questionable behavior from you. Your role is to correct your actions born from selfishness and lack of integrity.

SPIRITUAL CONNECTION

Ensuring your integrity through your accomplishments will enable appreciation for your sacrifices and achievements. As Christian leaders, we have a higher calling. As leaders in our workplace, community, and home, we must keep our eyes, heart, and mind focused on Jesus Christ to ensure we do not give in to temptation. Our actions must be of integrity and unquestionable. The apostle Paul says, Galatians 6:8, "For he who sows to his flesh will of the flesh reap corruption, but he who sows to the Spirit will of the spirit reap."[70]

Scripture tells us in the book of 1 John 2:15-17 the Father's love does not reside in the person who loves the flesh's desires. Sins like pride and disobedience get in the way of achieving your highest potential. Self-satisfaction and the search to win at all costs can be born out of insecurity.[71] King Saul's pride made him see David as an adversary versus an asset to his kingdom.[72] Insecurity can push away the talented people you need to strengthen the team. It can also drive away loved ones ready to support your growth.

To elevate your mindset, surround yourself with people who

---

[70] Galatians 6:8, New King James Version Bible.
[71] Muto, S. (2014) Virtues, *Your Christian Legacy*. Steubenville, OH: Emmaus Road Publishing.
[72] 1 Samuel 22, New King James Version Bible.

have ambition. The more time you spend with people content with average, the more comfortable you will feel giving up on your dreams. Be intentional about learning something new. In every failure, find learning. Stop complaining—you gain nothing from it. Pay attention to your words and be deliberate about being grateful for those who often get taken for granted. Dream more. Albert Einstein once said, "Imagine the possibilities—imagination will take you anywhere."

Stephen Covey once said, " "I'm not a product of my circumstance. I am a product of my decisions." She is the only one in her family to graduate high school and earn a master's degree. As if her education was not enough, she launched a successful business, and people acted on her wisdom. Yet the framed degrees, professional experience, and knowledge could not silence her insecurity of not being good enough. She spent over 30 years of her life trying to silence the insecurities through her achievements.

SPIRITUAL CONNECTION

Insecurities will find a way to creep into your mind and cause you to doubt yourself, causing, in many cases, anxiety. Anxiety attacks your mind causing destructive thoughts to genuine concerns. It's a constant battle. Remember, we must be intentional about elevating our mindset until it becomes the norm. It is a journey; you got this. We see in 2 Corinthians 10:5 we are to take every proud and untrue thought that stands up against the knowledge of God captive to the obedience of Christ. To take a thought captive means to govern your thoughts instead of letting the thoughts control you. It means to compare them to what scripture says and confirm their truth. 1 Corinthians 7:32 reminds us God wants us to be free from anxieties.

The reason toxic thoughts run rampant is we allow them to cause turmoil and chaos. We give our thoughts the power to control our emotions and, ultimately, our actions. However, the Apostle Paul leaves us a formula to fight back the toxic thoughts. Philippians 4:8 tells us to meditate on what is true, noble, just, pure, lovely, admirable, excellent, and worthy of praise. Do your thoughts pass this test? Challenging your thoughts will help you overcome adversity, and most importantly, you will be free to explore opportunities.

PRACTICAL EXERCISE

- List the toxic thoughts that run recklessly through your mind.
- Check to see if they are true, noble, just, pure, lovely, admirable, excellent, and worthy of praise for each thought. If they are not, ask yourself what is triggering these thoughts. As yourself, "Why?" five times until we break it down to the true root cause.

IN REAL LIFE: BREAKTHROUGHS SET US FREE

One day, while on a coaching session with my speaking coach, I had the most significant breakthrough of my life. My speaking coach asked me to incorporate the words "I'm smart" during a video shooting. To my unimaginable surprise, I froze; I struggled, and my eyes watered. The words could not come out of my mouth. My coach asked her, "Do you not think you are smart?" Immediately, tears began to flow from my eyes. It was as if I had opened the faucet. I was blinded to the self-limiting belief that I was not smart enough. So much so that I had never said the words, "I'm smart." The reality was the negative thoughts had held my talents captive for years. Sell-limiting beliefs planted long ago had built deep, strong roots. The roots were so deep I had learned to live with them and had forgotten who I was.

The recording session turned into a discovery session. When the coach asked me, "Who said you were not smart enough?" Memories popped up of one of my teachers and loved ones who had constantly repeated I was not smart enough. For a moment, I felt hopeless and scared of losing control. Yes, those words were said to me. However, my thoughts were not factual; I had proven that already. I was successful despite my self-limiting beliefs. So, why were these thoughts still haunting me? Simple, I had not faced them. I hid them inside my heart and chose to ignore them. While I was successful, I had not achieved my best performance. That day, I repeated "I am smart. I AM SMART" in between my tears. Today, I know my past doesn't define me, and I'm victorious. My potential was unlocked that day.

When I held my thoughts captive and realized they were not true, the chains that were holding me back from achieving greatness were broken. I am able to imagine and see things I have never seen before, and most importantly, I took action. What seemed impossible yesterday, today is possible.

SPIRITUAL CONNECTION

Luke 10 narrates. A woman named Martha welcomed Jesus into her home. And she had a sister called Mary, who sat at the Lord's feet and listened to his teaching. But Martha was distracted with much serving And she went up to him and said, "Lord, do you not care that my sister has left me to serve alone? Tell her then to help me." But the Lord answered her, "Martha, Martha, you are anxious and troubled about many things, but one thing is necessary. Mary has chosen the good portion, which will not be taken away from her."

Martha invited God into her life but failed to build a relationship with Him. Instead, Marth spent her energy on the small things that kept her busy but did not make a significant impact. Elevate your mindset and focus on the things that will transform you. It is easier to get distracted by the mindless stuff of life, like social media. When you have to choose between washing dishes or playing with your child, choose to play with your child. The dishes will still be there, but how your children feel at that moment will follow them for the rest of their lives. Trust me, we all need to learn how to relax and play again.

Refocus and choose to invest your energy wisely. How are you spending your energy? What thoughts are holding you back from unleashing your most talented gifts? Take action; without action, you cannot achieve success. An empty life can seem normal in a world filled with distractions. Self-reflection, failures, and struggles led me to the feet of Jesus. I know He is the key to my success. The Apostle Peter says, "Therefore gird up the loins of your mind, be sober, and rest your hope fully upon the grace that is to be brought to you at the revelation of Jesus Christ."

CHAPTER 4:

RESPECT

"You have been given a choice between war and dishonor.
You have chosen dishonor, and you will have war!"

~ Winston Churchill

Do you know how special you are? Self-respect is the ability to establish self-worth. To thrive, we must learn to love and respect ourselves as individuals.[73] How do you answer when asked if you love yourself or hate yourself? The answer lies in our actions. If we associate loving ourselves with respecting ourselves, why do you think we continue to break our promises and choose what diminishes us physically, mentally, emotionally, and spiritually? We all unconsciously disrespect ourselves and unintentionally weaken our worth at some point. The key is to catch ourselves and return to the truth; we are enough.

The inability to respect ourselves creates the "I'm not worthy" thoughts. You might not be saying it out loud, but your behavior

---

[73] Mackenzie, J. (2018). Knowing yourself and being worth knowing. *Journal of the American Philosophical Association*, 4(2), 243-261. doi:http://dx.doi.org.ezproxy. regent.edu/10.1017/apa.2018.19.

will state otherwise. Researchers call the lack of self-respect the "Why Try?" phenomenon. "Why Try?" results from self-stigma when we apply social stereotypes to ourselves and believe we are not worthy.[74] The emotional and behavioral consequences lead to a lack of self-respect. Respecting yourself means caring for the complete you. It means to be physically, emotionally, mentally, and spiritually healthy. The benefits are medically undeniable.

KEEP YOUR PROMISES

Integrity comes from the Latin word "integer," which means whole. Being whole includes your sense of commitment to what is wrong and right. Personal integrity is more than morality; it is about making us complete. Most of us think of integrity as external to us. However, self-integrity is the basis for ethical behavior. It is about honoring our word. If you lack integrity for your goals, you will cheat yourself out of your dreams. Living in integrity enables us to thrive with minimal stress and fewer complications. We have the power to be a person of integrity. Achieving self-integrity is liberating; it activates our power. Lying to ourselves may be easy, but the spirit rebukes it until the lack of self-integrity becomes a plague that tears us down from the inside out.

Integrity starts with how you honor yourself.

IN REAL LIFE: WE CAN HONOR SELF-INTEGRITY

"Mom, will you be at my soccer game this weekend?" my daughter anxiously asked. Without any thought, the words "Of

---

[74] Corrigan, P.W., Bink, A.B., Schmidt, A., Jones, N., & Rüsch, N. (2016). What is the impact of self-stigma? loss of self-respect and the "why try" effect. *Journal of Mental Health (Abingdon, England)*, 25(1), 10-15.

course, I will, darling," rolled off my tongue. But, once again, I broke my promise and missed the game. I promised myself I would make it home for dinner. Unfortunately, yet familiar, I had to take calls over the weekend because of a significant issue at the office that needed my attention. As I diligently worked through the late evening, the broken promises to my daughter tour my daughter's heart, and the promises I made to myself were no more.

My daughter waited, but by the time I arrived home, she was already in bed. The more I stressed, the more I calmed my anxiety by shopping online, forgetting I promised myself I would better manage my finances. The more I would lose my self-integrity, the more I used food as a coping mechanism, forgetting I vowed to care for my physical health. At the end of the long day, exhausted, I continuously skipped the time I had committed to spending with God. I was tired of working countless hours and breaking the promises to have a career discussion with my boss, but I again took no action towards what mattered most. My friends stopped calling, my daughter stopped inviting me to her games, and my husband about had enough.

Does it sound familiar? I was out of integrity. My daughter was convinced I loved work more than spending time with her, and I was sure I worked hard for her. I was about to lose the trust and respect of my family. Lack of self-integrity causes us to lose sight of what is truly important. It hurts and pushes away the true you and the ones you love. You see, self-integrity is like the battery on our phone, with each bar representing integrity. The phone can function with two bars and a red bar. The warnings are there, and we choose not to see them until the connection is lost.

I had a rude awakening and decided to make good on my promises. My daughter and I both cried with joy when I showed up at her game. I forgot how much I love to cheer for her or scream for her. Yes, guilty. I'm the loudest mother on the field. From that moment forward, I do not miss a game. My daughter and I aligned and Mom will be at the games. I may miss her practices, but I do not miss her games. While I admit, I still have to fulfill the promise I made to my husband to learn how to play golf. We picked out golf clubs, and I enjoyed shopping for women's golf wear together. I realized my eating habits and weight were out of control. Suppose I was to keep the promise to do everything in my power to stay healthy for my children, something needed to change. I did not want to fall out of integrity and begin the chronic self-integrity threat rollercoaster. I refuse to risk my self-integrity and once again hurt myself and those I love the most. I quickly realized I could not do it alone. I needed an accountability partner. The accountability partner encourages, supports, and pushes you when you absolutely do not want to do what you know needs to be done.

Lack of self-integrity is another barrier to change.[75] Living in integrity leads to increases in your self-worth and self-respect. Self-integrity will keep you focused on achieving the most significant achievement—being present with the people you love.

PRACTICAL EXERCISE

Think about the trigger points that push you out of goodness and pause before committing or breaking a commitment. Set

---

[75] Logel, C., Hall, W., Page, G. E., & Cohen, G. L. (2019). Why is it so hard to change? The role of self integrity threat and affirmation in weight loss. *European Journal of Social Psychology, 49*(4), 748–759. https://doi-org.ezproxy.regent. edu/10.1002/ejsp.2536

boundaries and be disciplined around them. Yes, the people benefiting from you will be upset, but you will be free to stand on your word. The law of truth should be within you so that you can walk in peace.[76]

Do not be so hard on yourself if you step out of integrity. Things happen, and you will break some promises. The key is to realize your actions and make them right.

- Are you practicing integrity with yourself?
- Are you keeping the promises you made to yourself?
- Do you put on an invisible mask every day to keep people from knowing the real you?

- **Make a List**
  - List the promises you have made and have not kept to yourself. Do not worry about the length of the list; keep writing.
  - List the promises you have made to loved ones and have not kept.
- Review the list and pay attention to your emotions; ask God for forgiveness, forgive yourself, and recommit your integrity. God desires to restore you.
- Take the opportunity to learn, to grow, and to get back into integrity.

- **Take Action**
  - What can you cross off the list for you today to get back into integrity?

---

[76] Malachi 2:6, New King James Version Bible.

- Is there someone you need to apologize to for not keeping a promise? If yes, make the call. If they are no longer with you, write a letter.
- There will be promises you cannot make right, but you can always apologize for not keeping your promise. If you absolutely cannot take action on anything on that list today. Now is the time to write a plan on how you will get back into integrity, beginning with fulfilling your promises or apologizing for not keeping your promise.

SPIRITUAL CONNECTION

King Solomon reminds us in Proverbs 12:22, "Lying lips are an abomination to the Lord. But those who deal truthfully are His delight." Think about those words for a moment. The Holy Spirit lives inside of us, and every time we are out of integrity, we deplete the energy that fuels us. Your actions must reflect what you value. If you value integrity in others, you must first be loyal to integrity with yourself. We cannot attract what we do not respect in ourselves. Step into integrity today by keeping the promise you made to yourself. You cannot achieve integrity if you are isolated from the truth. Trust God will give you what you need. It is time to take action and set free the power in you. When God is your priority, confusion is no more, integrity rules, time is enough, and peace reigns.

RESPECT YOUR LIFE

When you invest time in your physical, emotional, mental, and spiritual capacity, it leads to sustainable high performance. When we take care of ourselves, we can be better leaders and partners; we can be the light. It takes courage to invest time in your future self. Society rewards the here and now and celebrates activities while ignoring wholesome self-investment.

The Apostle Paul reminds us in I Corinthians 6:19-20 our body is the temple of the Holy Spirit. He exalts us to glorify God in our body and our spirit. Without our physical health, the rest of the body cannot function to its best capacity.

Physical wellness is the foundation of our welfare.[77] Our physical energy determines our ability to perform. Although you should always seek professional help for mental health, a healthy body can reduce depression, anxiety, and stress. It also improves our overall mood. A study conducted by the Harvard T.H. Chan School of Public Health determined a short 15-minute walk can reduce the risk of major depression by 26 percent.[78] Research also shows CEOs who are physically fit deliver higher profits.[79] Sadly, a staggering 40 percent of adults are obese, and 70 percent are considered overweight. Furthermore, the estimated cost of obesity in 2008 was $150 billion.[80]

ASK YOURSELF

- Do you find yourself energized in the morning after a cup of coffee and a donut?

- Do you regret it when you do not nourish your body with the healthy foods it needs?

---

[77] Loehr, J. & Schwartz, T. (2001). The making of a corporate athlete. *Harvard business review*, 79(1), 120-129.
[78] Publishing, H. (n.d.). More evidence that exercise can boost mood. Retrieved January 12, 2021, from https://www.health.harvard.edu/mind-and-mood/more-evidence-that-exercise-can-boost-mood
[79] Vijayaraghavan, K. (2015, Feb 09). Why staying fit is an imperative for business heads getting older & seeking to stay at the top [panache]. *The Economic Times*.
[80] Baker, P. & Norton, L. (2019). Fat Loss Forever: How to Lose Fat and Keep it Off. *Biolayne*. 3.

- Does the attire you wear make your confidence level drop or increase?
- Are you fighting for energy by the middle of the day?

You are not alone if you answered yes to most of the questions. If it were easy to prioritize your health in a society that does not put you first, everyone would do it. Yet, the truth still stands, we cannot give our best when our physical body is fighting for power amid stress, shame, long days, family, and critical work decisions. Self-respect starts with taking care of our physical body—we owe it to ourselves. You owe it to those who love you.

For most women, physical appearance is a priority. Women do not like talking about it, but it must be said because we are losing ourselves in the process. By the time we realize we have lost ourselves, we feel ashamed. Shame dims our light and makes us alienate ourselves from others. It is like mold; it grows in the dark. It pushes you away from loving you. Studies show "shame is a highly aversive emotional experience that is integrally associated with avoidance and withdrawal tendencies."[81] People who experience shame will typically walk with collapsed shoulders, with their heads almost bowed down and eyes facing down to avoid making eye contact with others.

DIETING: LET'S TALK ABOUT IT

Dieting is part of our culture; let us face it head-on. What do you think of when you think of the word "diet?" Most people are used to drastically restricting calories, cutting out entire food

---

[81] McGregor, H.A., & Elliot, A.J. (2005). The shame of failure: Examining the link between fear of failure and shame. *Personality & Social Psychology Bulletin*, 31(2), 218-231. doi:10.1177/0146167204271420.

groups, skipping meals, feeling very hungry, low energy, and having an "end" date in mind. It seems like a new fad diet or miracle weight loss pill is marketed to people desperate to lose weight every week. There are cult-like followings of a slew of en vogue diets promising quick results, including Keto, Intermittent Fasting, the Carnivore Diet, the Mediterranean Diet, and even the Blood Type Diet. We all love to reason, "If X diet worked for her, it would work for me." Whereas, the real question should be, "Is it healthy?" "Will this diet respect and nourish my body appropriately?" "Is it sustainable?"

Supplements offer an easy out, quick fix, and instant gratification to people who want to lose weight "yesterday" and, let's face it, do not want to put in the work. Many of us are unwilling to implement the lifestyle changes, hard work, and discipline necessary. It is no wonder the Global Weight Loss Supplement Market continues to grow and will reach $40 billion by 2024.

A vast majority of us know the key to physical health is moving more and eating less calorie-dense processed foods. When we prioritize our health, we decrease the risk for cardiovascular disease, cancer, diabetes, improve quality of life, and let's not forget about the obvious one—looking and feeling sexy.[82] Given the benefits of weight loss, we would be hard-pressed to find someone who hasn't been on a diet at some point in their life. So, why does the obesity rate continue to climb?

It turns out people aren't actually "bad" at losing weight. The majority who attempt to diet are successful at losing weight. The real problem lies in keeping the weight off. Although the sources

---

[82] Baker, P. & Norton, L. (2019). Fat Loss Forever: How to Lose Fat and Keep it Off. *Biolayne.* 5-6.

vary, it is consistently believed between 50 percent to 70 percent of people regain all the weight within one year of weight loss. Within three years, the numbers are even more troubling—95 percent of people will have gained it all back.[83] Only 5 percent of dieters successfully keep the weight off. The other 95 percent are sadly once again feeling like a failure, in shame, and wondering how we got there. What sets the 5 percent apart from the unsuccessful majority? The answer lies in various physiological, psychological, and sociological reasons. However, it all leads to the choices we make, our thoughts, and how much we genuinely want the best for ourselves.

Anyone who starts an extreme diet will notice it's relatively easy to lose weight rapidly at first, but eventually, weight loss slows down. Why? "Metabolic adaptation stops weight loss in its tracks because what was once an energy deficit eventually becomes energy balance (calories consumed now equals calories expended) and weight loss stops unless a further restriction is imposed."[84] Let me stay real. The diet industry does not care if you keep the weight off. It only cares if you buy their product and lose weight in the short term.

The answer to sustainable healthy weight loss is respecting yourself and your body enough to make slow, sustainable changes that work for you. The keyword here is sustainable. Because it works for you, it does not mean it will work for me. The best diet is one that is sustainable to you long-term. No one diet is more successful than the other in keeping the weight off—the key is lasting behavioral change. You may have heard

---

[83] Baker, P. & Norton, L. (2019). Fat Loss Forever: How to Lose Fat and Keep it Off. *Biolayne*. 4
[84] Baker, P. & Norton, L. (2019). Fat Loss Forever: How to Lose Fat and Keep it Off. *Biolayne*. 24.

the Chinese proverb, "A journey of 1,000 miles begins with a single step." You have the choice every day you wake up to take a step closer or farther from your goals and values.

Next time you are tempted to regain your health using the quick-fix strategies promised by diet-culture, ask yourself, "How did that work for me last time?" If you can honestly answer, "Not well," you may consider trying a different approach, such as flexible dieting. Flexible dieting works by creating a modest calorie deficit. You reduce your calories and eliminate the thinking of "good" and "bad" foods. Much like life, our diets are never going to be "perfect," nor is it helpful to beat yourself up if you fail to eat "perfectly." What happens when people fall off the proverbial diet wagon? More likely than not, they end up binging and feeling guilty for overeating, vowing to "start over again" tomorrow. This type of thinking can lead to a vicious binge-restrict cycle and is counterproductive to reaching your goals. The best kind of diet accommodates your lifestyle and nourishes your mental well-being, as well.

Eating healthy nourishes your physical, emotional, and mental health. If your physical health fails, there is nothing left. There is no you.

SPIRITUAL CONNECTION

Today, more than ever before, we are conditioned to expect instant gratification. Amazon Prime, smartphones, and "buy now, pay later plans" are just a few of the ways society conditions and appeases our need for speed. But what does the Bible say about waiting? Jesus was tempted by Satan three times, but each time he resisted—knowing the end game. David didn't become king overnight The Israelites wandered the wilderness for 40 years before entering the Promised Land. Also, Sarah was 90 years old when she became pregnant with Isaac. What is the point? Our physical health is a journey, not an overnight miracle.

Unfortunately, speed takes priority over patience today. Remember, patience is one of the fruits of the spirit. Yet, culture continues to push us against such a valuable fruit. In a society touting fast results, it is counter-cultural to be patient. Stand your ground, do what is sustainable, do what will work for you long term.

IN REAL LIFE: WE OWN HOW WE SPEND OUR ENERGY

At 40 years of age, my husband and I welcomed home our first child. Two children later and a demanding executive role, I spent my energy caring for our family, working, serving the community, and taking classes toward my doctorate. Eating unhealthy snacks and drinking large amounts of caffeine kept me going until it did not. During a routine lab test, I discovered my health was deteriorating fast. I was stressed, depressed, overweight, and my lab results were all bright red. Once, a marathon runner, avid hiker, and outgoing individual who loved to entertain company, now ashamed of my body, hid behind the excuse that I was too busy. And guess I was busy, busy working on self-destruction, that is. I vividly remember the words of my doctor, "If you do not love yourself enough, do it for your children because you will not be around for them if you continue on this lifestyle." The words were harsh, they made me angry, and I hated her for saying those words to me. But I could not deny what the doctor told me was the truth. I had lost my self-respect; I had forgotten how to love myself. The lack of care for my physical well-being affected my emotional and mental health. As a result, it negatively impacted my relationships, marriage, and children.

PRACTICAL EXERCISE

That day I went home and made a list of the five things that matter to me the most; faith, family, wellness, career, and relationships.

- List the five things that matter to you the most.

1. Family
2. friends
3. physical wellness / exercise
4. mental wellness
5. being a blessing to others

- Then categorized under "crystal balls" and "rubber balls." If it falls, does it break, or does it bounce back?

It was then I realized if I lost my health, nothing else mattered because I would not be around to enjoy my children or shine in my career.

Although I knew it wouldn't be easy, this was the catalyst I needed to make a change. I eat everything, but I practice cognitive restraint by swapping calorie-dense foods for higher protein and whole foods. I eat sweets because I love them; I just limit the portion size. I also hired a personal trainer as an accountability partner to ensure I do not skip my fitness routine—giving it the same priority as my other responsibilities. But most importantly, I persevered through the soreness. I persevered through the fatigue. I persevered through the tears. I do not quit, even want to stop; it has made all the difference.

To enjoy the fruits of your labor, you must invest time in your physical health. Discipline is critical to achieving physical fitness because motivation will not be enough. Bad habits are not easy to break. It will take shifting your energy to power a better you. "Above the physical health rests emotional health, then mental acuity, and at the top, a sense of purpose. The Ideal Performance State—peak performance under pressure—is achieved when all levels work together."[85]

BODY SHAME

Women in the United States are disproportionately affected by body image concerns linked to eating disorders and depression.[86] For years many have complained about the body images on the media as being unrealistic. The consequences of weight stigma and discrimination include lost educational and employment opportunities, inadequate medical treatment, and even unfair jury decisions.[87] In just one week of recording their experiences, over 70 percent of obese women said they were bullied or teased for their weight.[88] As you might imagine, bullying overweight people does not inspire them to lose weight and can have the opposite effect.

[85] Loehr, J. & Schwartz, T. (2001). The making of a corporate athlete. *Harvard business review*, 79(1), 120-129.
[86] Velez, B.L., Campos, I.D., & Moradi, B. (2015). Relations of sexual objectification and racist discrimination with Latina Women's body image and mental health. *The Counseling Psychologist, 43*(6), 906-935. doi:10.1177/0011000015591287.
[87] Mann PhD, T. (2015). Secrets From the Eating Lab: The Science of Weight Loss, the Myth of Willpower, and Why You Should Never Diet Again. *HarperCollins*. 159.
[88] Mann PhD, T. (2015). Secrets From the Eating Lab: The Science of Weight Loss, the Myth of Willpower, and Why You Should Never Diet Again. *HarperCollins*. 163.

Perhaps our culture promoting body image as the utmost concern for women is part of the problem. In a sad turn of events, research shows young women's primary concerns for self-improvement in the 1890s focused on character—they wanted to be kinder and do well in school. One hundred years later, historian Joan Jacobs Brumberg found the same age group's primary concern was improving their body appearance. How does one improve on their physical appearance? The answer almost always involves a fad, whether weight loss, surgery, fitness hack, or a beauty product. It is not a secret that industries profit from women's insecurities.

Exercise is proven to do many wonderful things for both a woman's mental and physical health. It becomes unhealthy when you set a goal to reshape your body into one that is unachievable. Photoshopped images encourage less self-care daily instead of inspiring women to build healthier and more capable bodies.

Studies have found negative beliefs about one's appearance can cause Body Dysmorphic Disorder (BDD). BDD is an extreme obsession with a perceived defect or flaw in appearance that others cannot see.[89] Studies show people with BDD "tend to have poor insight and even suffer from delusions of reference."

Focusing on ourselves does not always translate into self-love. It also can mean we hate ourselves so much that we spend a tremendous amount of time fixated on our perceived flaws. If we hate our body image, we may be obsessed with what we eat until we are no longer fun to be around. Yes, we should be intentional about what we eat, but being deliberate

---

[89] Markey, C., & Gillen, M. (2015;2016;). *Body image and mental health, Encyclopedia of Mental Health,* Elsevier Science & Technology, 2015. *ProQuest Ebook Central,* http://ebookcentral.proquest.com/lib/regent-ebooks/detail.action?docID=4003864. Created from regent-ebooks on 2021-01-12 08:00:36.

and obsessed are two different things Many women undergo invasive cosmetic surgery; others fall into eating disorders, others become addicted to drugs and alcohol. While there are many reasons for falling into addiction, self-respect and self-love can prevent you from falling into this suppressed area. Our self-limiting beliefs will keep us from loving ourselves and seeing us worthy of being loved the way we deserve.[90] Thoughts of not being able to perform can cause social anxiety disorder.[91] Self-respect leads you to learn more about yourself and love you enough to care for a better you. A fit woman comes in different shapes and forms; the key is to build your physical capacity, not to look like an unrealistic magazine model. Keep in mind that a healthy body is often much different from the one our culture paints as aesthetically ideal.

To ensure we can spend our energy the right way, we must practice self-control. We must be able to balance our flaws with self-love. Our relationship with ourselves matters because self-respect will influence our behavior and those we invite into our lives. "Self-respect thus has an aspirational dimension to it insofar as it requires that we strive to set worthwhile ends for ourselves and that we be careful about how we pursue those ends."[92]

The shortcuts will cut your life short. You are beautifully and wonderfully made.

[90] Mackenzie, J. (2018). Knowing yourself and being worth knowing. *Journal of the American Philosophical Association*, 4(2), 243-261. doi: http://dx.doi.org.ezproxy.regent.edu/10.1017/apa.2018.19
[91] Markey, C. & Gillen, M. (2015;2016;). *Body image and mental health, Encyclopedia of Mental Health*, Elsevier Science & Technology, 2015. *ProQuest Ebook Central*, http://ebookcentral.proquest.com/lib/regent-ebooks/detail.action?
[92] Mackenzie, J. (2018). Knowing yourself and being worth knowing. *Journal of the American Philosophical Association*, 4(2), 243-261. doi: http://dx.doi.org.ezproxy.regent.edu/10.1017/apa.2018.19

SPIRITUAL CONNECTION

The Bible warns against the perils of worshipping vanity. On 1 Peter 3, we are reminded of what is precious in God's eyes: "The beauty of a gentle and quiet spirit, not the braiding of hair and the putting on of gold jewelry or clothing you wear." Scripture does not condemn women making themselves feel beautiful. The problem is when it becomes the main focus, as it can be a slippery slope because you can look good on the outside and be rotting on the inside. Still, the increasingly visual and digitally altered world we live in values fleeting outer appearances over inner health.

IN REAL LIFE: OUR VALUES DECIDE WHAT IS HEALTHY

Growing up in rural Nebraska, Penelope was raised by two hard-working. She excelled in athletics and academics and received a full scholarship to a four-year university. Penelope was set up for success and positioned to succeed. The only problem, Penelope did not have confidence in herself. She conformed to the unrealistic beauty standards she saw portrayed in the media. Although it may seem bizarre, it is not uncommon.

Penelope started high school in 2003—a coming of age when everything was hypersexualized. Girls Gone Wild was promoted on late-night infomercials, and young girls shopped at Victoria's Secret in an attempt to imitate the impossibly thin models promoted in the fashion shows and advertising. Four years earlier, at the age of 17, Britney Spears posed for the cover of *Rolling Stone* in her underwear. Low-rise hip-hugging jeans were in style and fit Penelope's adolescent body. It wasn't until she went through puberty that pants did not quite fit her body type, and she started skipping meals—avoiding the lunchroom at noon so that no one would notice. This only led to more disordered eating as she would starve herself all day to later binge. Like many other women today, Penelope's self-confidence was dictated by a number on the scale. She became obsessed with trying to weigh an arbitrary number on the scale. This behavior continued into her early 20s as Penelope was mortified by her first boyfriend telling her she was "pleasantly plump."

Unfortunately, disordered eating and poor body image are too common and impact a women's self-confidence. According to the National Eating Disorders Association, more than 13 percent of girls have suffered from an eating disorder by age 20. Images in magazines and movies fueled Penelope's insecurities. Today, that pressure has been ramped up with the rise of social media and people like us attached to our smartphones 24/7 in a sad attempt to seek validation for our insecurities through social media. Sadly, brilliant women are affected by social media insecurities. In her memoir, Gabrielle Korn talks about the "Instagram Generation" about her time spent in the fashion and beauty industry.

"The platform gives everyone—celebrity or otherwise—total control over the images of themselves that are published for the world to see, but in reality, once we have that control, we haven't found ourselves implementing the lessons we've learned about the way Photoshop and runway models have affected Western female self-esteem; instead, we use filters, and other apps to change pretty much whatever you want on your face and body."[93]

[93] Korn, G. (2021). *Everybody (Else) Is Perfect: How I Survived Hypocrisy, Beauty, Clicks, and Likes,* New York, NY: Atria Books.

It is no secret that social platforms are the highlight reel of people's lives. Although we are aware images are often photoshopped, it doesn't stop us from feeling insecure after looking at these images. Eve was the first woman fooled by Satan's lies—and not the last. Social media can become damaging, exhausting, addicting, and all-encompassing if not kept in check. Although the internet can bring us together, it also has the power to tear our self-confidence and healthy mindset. It is imperative to pay attention to the content you consume—if it makes you feel worse about yourself, you might want to ask yourself if you're voluntarily feeding yourself poison.

Social media can become damaging, exhausting, addicting, and all-encompassing if not kept in check.

Today, there is a blurred line between female empowerment and perfectionism. Women's media is scrambling to be more positive and inclusive while reporting on fashion and beauty. Although an estimated 30 million people in the United States struggle with eating disorders, over 70 percent would not seek treatment because of the stigma. "In this golden age of female empowerment, we're not supposed to have eating disorders anymore. It's not cool to hate your body. Most public eye women are obligated to promote a message of self-love, vulnerability, and true self. Culturally, we're all about 'wellness' and defining what works for us as individuals. Yet, studies show that eating disorder rates are not decreasing, but rising."[94]

Like everything, there is a spectrum. It is up to you and your values to decide what is a healthy level of focus on appearance for you—while keeping in mind beauty is fleeting, deriving your

---

[94] Korn, G. (2021). *Everybody (Else) Is Perfect: How I Survived Hypocrisy, Beauty, Clicks, and Likes,* NY, NY: Atria Books.

confidence and self-worth solely from your appearance will not end well. In an eye-opening essay on the body positivity movement for Racked, Amanda Mull writes, "To have a body that's widely reviled and discriminated against and love it anyway in the face of constant cultural messaging about your flaws is subversive."[95]

Diana was born in Chester, England. Her family was part of a Christian movement called the Plymouth Brethren. They did not require ministers, only guest speakers, as their guide was the Bible alone. Although Diana spent several days a week in church, and she attended public school in a primarily secular community. She often felt ostracized by the church's rules because they varied so wildly from her peers' upbringing. Keep in mind this was 40 years ago—before the advent of social media and smartphones. Diana grew up without a television in her home—the Brethren had another name for it, "devil-vision." Raised under artificial religious practices, she couldn't cut, color, or perm her hair and wouldn't dream of wearing makeup.

Diana went on to join an Evangelical Church in America, where she would raise her six children. The church's primary focus for women was developing their character and serving others. Although she chose not to stay within the confines of such a ritualistic church, she can now see how her strict upbringing helped shape her into the woman she is today. The idea of worrying about her outward appearance is a foreign concept to Diana. She never doubted herself or suffered from low self-esteem based on her appearance and body image.

I imagine you would be hard-pressed to find a modern woman

[95] Korn, G. (2021). *Everybody (Else) Is Perfect: How I Survived Hypocrisy, Beauty, Clicks, and Likes,* NY, NY: Atria Books.

who hasn't struggled with body image given our culture's obsession with thinness and outward beauty. However, we can learn from Diana. Her character pushes her to be better without shame. Although rejecting society's standard of beauty will be almost impossible, it is essential to keep it in check, both for our mental and physical health. Perhaps then we could better look at others without insecurities or judgment.

Diana raised her three daughters with the same values and apathetic attitude toward outward appearance as she was raised. The only difference was they had more access to mainstream forms of media, such as television, magazines, and the beginnings of social media. Somewhat surprisingly, all three daughters struggled with negative body image in their young adulthood—often resorting to unhealthy measures to stay thin. The eldest passed out at work from lack of calories after partaking in a crash diet to lose weight in an effort to come back to high school the following school year as thin as her peers. The middle daughter ended her sports career when she developed a stress fracture from a lack of calcium in her foot. The youngest daughter let peers and fashion magazines dictate what they thought her body should look like. Her youngest daughter would buy clothes in a smaller size to motivate her to diet. It is scary to believe even in a home with the best of role models and arguably minimal media presence in the middle of rural America, all three women experienced the unspeakable pressures of society to conform to a certain standard.

PRACTICAL EXERCISE

To build and preserve self-respect, we must have compassion for ourselves. Look at ourselves the way God sees us, as the apple of His eye.

- **Make a list.** What are three things you love about yourself?

1. _I am a kind person_
2. _I genuinely care about others._
3. _____

- **Take Action.** Add the three things you love about yourself as a calendar reminder each day. Sometimes we need a reminder when we cannot see the beauty we possess.
- **Do not seek the approval of others.** You will never be able to make everyone happy. Know God loves you, and He died for you so that you can be set free.
- **Create a support system.** A support system can include professional help, a mentor, accountability partner, or a friend you trust to help you on your journey. No situation is too big or too small. Building a support system will allow you to fall in love with the greatness in you.
- **Be zealous about yourself!** Reinforce what you love about yourself each day. Strength is not a destiny but a journey of determination.

TOXIC RELATIONSHIPS

Self-respect is more than physical. It is about the people we invite into our lives as well. Toxic relationships are draining, and often their negative energy influences our well-being. One toxic relationship has the power to impact your emotional and mental state negatively. It takes courage to recognize you are engaging in a toxic relationship and even more courage to walk away. Have you ever heard of the doormat treatment? The doormat treatment is when you feel you cannot stand up for yourself and others take advantage of you. An example of doormat treatment is when someone makes you the office or family joke while you listen in embarrassment and say nothing.

Enabling and allowing this behavior also corresponds to a lack of self-respect. It is imperative to find the courage not to be submissive before degrading treatment.[96] Suppose you cannot speak up about this type of behavior in a work environment. I would recommend you begin to look for other employment. I can give you a list of other legal measures you can take, but your mental well-being is worth more than gold. While it is easier said than done, the reality is the longer you stay in this type of situation, the harder it will be to leave and the more damage it will do to you.

Some of us may experience the feeling of the doormat treatment when we forgive a person who continues to hurt us. Remember, forgiving does not mean reconciliation. In some cultures, people say forgiving an unpaid debt reflects weakness. However, there is no denying over and over; studies confirm forgiveness increases greater personal satisfaction.[97]

IN REAL LIFE: WE CAN FORGIVE AND THRIVE

She was intelligent, beautiful, confident, and in her last semester of college. She met a handsome young man who also said he loved God, and she fell in love. One day she woke up feeling unworthy, and she could not figure out how she got there. Throughout the years, the subtle comments and some

[96]Kellenberger, J. Dying to Self and Detachment, Taylor & Francis Group, 2016. *ProQuest Ebook Central*, https://ebookcentral-proquest-com.ezproxy.regent.edu/lib/regent-ebooks/detail.action?docID=956308.

[97] Luchies, L B., Finkel, E.J., McNulty, J.K., & Kumashiro, M. (2010). The doormat effect: When forgiving erodes self-respect and self-concept clarity. *Journal of Personality and Social Psychology*, 98(5), 734−749.

not so indirect made by the man she loved had finally tipped the glass over, and she found herself lost. "You should wear your hair differently." "You got promoted because you are a woman." "No one would love you as I do." "I do not even know why I'm with you." She did not understand how she allowed someone to pollute her mind and make her believe such things about herself. Every time she tried to walk away, he would apologize, start going to church, and she would forgive him. She fell into the same trap over and over. He knew what hurt her, motivated her, and drove her. Instead of using it for good, he used it to break her into pieces from the inside out. After many failures, she learned forgiving did not mean reconciliation. Through supportive friendships, prayer, grieving, and the power of the Holy Spirit, she was able to move on.

SPIRITUAL CONNECTION

God has a purpose for you, and the enemy will do everything it can to keep you from meeting your purpose. The reality is the devil does not show up with a red cape and horns. The enemy also knew what she found attractive and blinded her with the flesh and words. He was handsome and said he was a Christian, but he did not live a Christian life. Remember, a man of God strives each day to have the character of God. A man who truly loves God will love you because God is love. Do not be deceived; anyone can say they are a movie star and only played an extra.

Toxic relationships are all around us, and how we engage them determines their impact on our lives. We must recognize that we will never change another individual; it is not our job to change them. However, it is your responsibility to understand what attracts you to toxic relationships.

IN REAL LIFE: TRUE LOVE CAN BE FOUND

She was young when her daddy had passed to be with the Lord—losing her first love created a paralyzing fear that kept her in shackles for years in a toxic relationship. She thought if she only tried a little harder, he would change. Insecurities kept her in a toxic relationship and robbed her of some of the best years of her life.

She loved God and asked God to show her a sign, and she would walk away from the relationship. Sign after sign, she ignored it until she stopped praying, stopped seeking God, and ultimately lost herself in depression. She says her mother's faith and prayers saved her and brought her to the feet of Jesus once again. She was freed from her fear and safely walked away from the relationship. Today, she experiences God's love through her husband and their four children. She now knows no one loves her more than God does.

Recognizing the signs of a toxic relationship is vital to enabling self-respect. Sometimes it is hard for us to see the toxicity and the excuses we make up for them. Engaging with people you trust and love to give you feedback is essential. But most importantly, paying attention to the signs God gives you and taking action to remove yourself from toxic relationships will allow you to live a joyful life. Here are some behaviors to look for in a toxic person.

- A family member or friend continually points out your flaws with the motive to hurt you.
- A partner who mentally abuses you and in the same breath tells you, "I love you."
- needy friend who continuously drains you emotionally but does not support you when you need a friend.

- A person whose words and actions cannot be trusted.
- An individual who continues to abuse others mentally and physically.
- An individual who constantly brings up their financial status with the intent that you support them.
- A person who avoids conflict and blames others for their mistakes.

IN REAL LIFE: FRIENDSHIPS ARE NOT ALL CREATED EQUAL

Sometimes poisonous friendship may be disguised as a good friend. "I love you" were the last words he said to her. Their relationship was not perfect, but it was all she knew. Moments later, he died in a crash. Grief consumed her. Her friends, eager to help her, would take her out drinking until drinking was the only thing that made her happy. Making a fool of herself, her friends would pick her up from the floor and take her home. She made them laugh in her drunken state, but depression and addiction now controlled her. Toxic friends find humor in your misery even when they think they are only helping you. It is our responsibility to surround ourselves with people who have our best interest. Difficulty will come and we will need special friends in our lives. Invite friends into your life who will cry with you versus get drunk with you. Nourish the friends who will sit with you in your silence and laugh with you in your joy. Practicing self-control in all you do will nourish a better you. Ephesians 5:18 reminds us to not be filled by things that control or destroy us but instead allow the Holy Spirit to guide you.

Toxic relationships are like viruses. Lack of self-respect puts you at a higher risk of attracting toxic relationships. Studies found that every happy friend increases our chances of happiness by 11 percent. Still, we only need one toxic friend to double our miserable chances.[98]

Toxic relationships will make you doubt your worth until you drink the poison.

SPIRITUAL WELL-BEING

During Whitney Houston's eulogy, Kevin Costner said, "Arguably the biggest pop star in the world wasn't sure if she was good enough. She didn't think she looked right. There were a thousand things to her that seemed wrong. Despite her success and worldwide fame, the Whitney I knew still wondered, 'Am I good enough? Am I pretty enough? Will they like me?' It was the burden that made her great and the part that caused her to stumble in the end."[99]

It is time to activate respect and love for who you are. It is time to see yourself the way God sees you, a conqueror. You can be in the best physical shape, be rich and famous and still be spiritually weak.

More recently, the importance of spiritual well-being has become more significant. Why? Because spirituality has everything to do with leadership effectiveness.[100] Spirituality is not religious rituals. Religion separates people; it is human-made, while spirituality is associated with your relationship and

[98] Garello, M. (2019, April 20). *La negatividad es contagiosa: Rodéate de personas que saquen lo mejor de ti.* El Estado Digital. https://www.elestadodigital. com/2019/04/20/la-negatividad-es-contagiosa-rodeate-de-personas-que-saquen-lo-mejor-de-ti/

[99] *Transcripts Whitney Houston: Her Life, Her Music.* (2012, February 18). CNN Transcripts. http://transcripts.cnn.com/TRANSCRIPTS/1202/18/se.03.html

[100] Reave, L. (2005). Spiritual values and practices related to leadership effectiveness. *The Leadership Quarterly,* 16(5), 655-687.

connection with God [101] However, to grow spiritually, one must be disciplined in seeking a relationship with Him. Yet, discipline alone will never be enough to achieve spiritual growth.

Nevertheless, our discipline to seek God will put us in a position where God can work in us and strengthen our spiritual well-being. "Holistic spiritual disciplines are acts of loving obedience that we offer to God steadily and consistently to be used for whatever work God purposes to do in and through our lives."[102] Richard Foster, a christian theologian, outlines spiritual disciplines to enable your spiritual growth. Below are some of the disciplines that have helped me in my journey to spiritual well-being.

- **Meditation through prayer and reflection of scripture.** Meditation is not about achieving a clear mind for a few minutes or memorizing scripture. It is about intentionally connecting with God. Meditation with God requires intimacy. It is about removing the competing priorities in your life for a moment with your creator. Meditation is about growing closer to God, the only one who can give you peace in a time of chaos.

- **Fasting.** Fast from those things that we have accustomed to worship and place before God. Fasting is between you and God, not for the whole world to know. People typically give up food for a certain period of time. However, social media can be the one thing you worship that keeps you from listening to God's voice. What and how you fast are

---

[101] Reave, L. (2005). Spiritual values and practices related to leadership effectiveness. *The Leadership Quarterly,* 16(5), 655-687.
[102] Mulholland, M.R., Jr. (1993). *Invitation to a journey: A road map for spiritual formation.* Downers Grove, IL: InterVarsity.

between you and God. God knows what you value and what you are offering. When you seek validation from the world, do not expect recognition from God.

- **Studying scripture.** Study the scriptures with the intent to see it through God's eyes and removing the limits we put on God, not intending to prove our point.
- **Submit to God.** Submitting yourself to God is probably the most challenging discipline to achieve. Submitting to God is our willingness to be open to His will and guidance.[103] Many of us say we are willing to surrender our life to Jesus, but we take control of the things that matter to us the most. Unfortunately, we do not give God complete control. We try to fix our loved ones, finances, depression, or addiction because we are reluctant to do what He wants us to do.
- **Service to others versus servicing ourselves.** Too many do good deeds to receive "likes" and praise for themselves. When we serve others for God's glory, we put aside our pride to boast about our works.
- **Confession.** Confessing your secrets, fears, failures, and weakness to God and others allows you to experience forgiveness and holistic healing.
- **Worshipping God.** This is one of my favorite things to do. There are different ways to worship Him. You can worship God through music, words, adoration, and your testimony.
- **An intimate relationship with God.** This enables you to understand God's purpose in your life.
- **Speak life.** It brings life to you and your circumstances.

---

[103] Mulholland, M.R., Jr. (1993). *Invitation to a journey: A road map for spiritual formation.* Downers Grove, IL: InterVarsity.

SPIRITUALITY AND LEADERSHIP

Spiritual leadership and transformational leadership are directly linked, according to research.[104] However, "workplace spirituality research has sidestepped religion by focusing on the function of belief rather than its substance."[105] Spiritual leaders inspire, make ethical decisions, are trustworthy, respect others, cultivate positive relationships, reduce turnover, increase productivity, and improve those around them. Spiritual leadership does not overburden others by preaching religion. Instead, we lead by example through spiritual values like integrity, proven critical in leadership effectiveness. For countless years business leadership and spirituality have been separated. However, research can no longer deny the importance of spirituality in the workplace.[106]

We read earlier your spiritual capacity "provides a powerful source of motivation, determination, and endurance."[107] As christian leaders, spiritual health starts with the conviction of sin, receiving Jesus Christ as our savior, and sanctification.[108] Sanctification refers to the process in which there is no sin separating an individual from God. Humanity fails to understand that we do not fight against flesh and blood but spiritual principles. Spiritual powers are something that we all should take seriously.

---

[104] Crossman, J. (2010). Conceptualizing spiritual Leadership in secular organizational contexts and its relation to a transformational, servant, and environmental Leadership. *Leadership & Organizational Development.*
[105] Lynn, M.L., Naughton, M.J., & Vanderveen, S. (2009). Faith at work scale (FWS): Justification, development, and validation of a measure of Judaea-Christian religion in the workplace: *JBE. Journal of Business Ethics,* 85(2), 227-243.
[106] Reave, L. (2005). Spiritual values and practices related to leadership effectiveness. *The Leadership Quarterly,* 16(5), 655-687.
[107] Loehr, J. & Schwartz, T. (2001). The making of a corporate athlete. *Harvard business review,* 79(1), 120-129.
[108] Gyertson, D. (2009). I *Believe in the Holy Spirit One Pilgrim's Response to Contemporary Beliefs About and Practices Attributed to the Work and Ministry of the Holy Spirit.*

The Holy Spirit's presence in our lives is more critical than ever. While science now supports your spiritual well-being is essential for your overall health, Scripture confirmed this for us long ago. The Apostle Luke reminds us, "But you shall receive power when the Holy Spirit has come upon you." Have you experienced the power of the Holy Spirit? If you have not, I invite you to seek him with your whole heart. The transformation is undeniable.

Do you really know how critical your spiritual health is to your leadership capability? As a leader, you can inspire individuals, teams, cities, and nations. A christian leader powered by the Holy Spirit transforms more than businesses and goes beyond achieving their best self; they transform generations. As christian leaders, our dependency comes entirely from Christ. It should not come from our profession, education, friends, or even our loved ones. Our loved ones will fail us, and our credentials will no longer be relevant one day. When the world fails us, and it will, our spiritual health must be anchored in God to allow us to navigate the rough waters with peace. Let us be clear—apart from God, our spiritual health weakens.

Being made in God's image has its perks. When you have an intimate relationship with God, your spiritual senses are activated. When your spiritual senses are activated, it gives you the capacity to experience things at a different level.[109] Your spiritual eyes will allow you to see what is in front of you through a spiritual lens beyond the natural.

In the book of II Kings 6, we learn about the servant terrified of the army surrounding the city coming to destroy Elisha, a man of God. The servant's fear did not allow him to see what Elisha saw,

---

[109] Haapalainen, A. (2016). Spiritual senses as a resource. Temenos, 52(2), 289-311. doi:10.33356/temenos.60308.

but Elisha asked God to open his eyes so he could see. However, Elisha calmly said to his servant, "Do not fear, for those who are with us are more than those who are with them." Through his spiritual eyes, Elisha was able to see the army of God with chariots of fire backing him up against the earthly army. Elisha saw God's protection, and both escaped without harm.

Spiritual discernment can come from visions. On January 12, 2020, I had a vision. The sky was gray and black as far as the eye could see. Then suddenly, lighting, hail, and massive heavy raindrops poured from the clouds. Despite the storm, a white flower grew and produced more fruit. As it rose through the cracked floor, red seeds fell to the ground, causing other flowers to bloom. The darker the skies became, the stronger the flower grew. At the time, it did not make sense until the COVID-19 pandemic hit shortly after.

The church of God must continue its work to plant seeds for His glory. During the pandemic, H.E.R.A.C.T. began to take shape. Women were broken and in need of healing. While everyone was going virtual, God kept the January 12, 2020 vision on my mind and replay. From this vision, the ACTivate H.E.R.A.C.T. Conference was born. Many said moving forward with an in-person conference was reckless, but when God tells you to do His will, well, you do it. You do it knowing He will make the impossible possible. That is His specialty; after all, He is the creator of all things. Taking the appropriate precautions, everyone in attendance stayed safe and healthy. When you take care of His work, He takes care of you. What seems impossible becomes possible, and others will never understand. Remember this—God's purpose in you is not the same as God's purpose for them. Please note if you do not have God's support, do not move forward with your actions. If he calls you to do the work, He will protect you and straighten the crooked places.

On September 5, 2020, the ACTivate Conference received 62 women from around the United States. From doctors, multi-million-dollar business owners, attorneys, executives, homemakers to convicts who came out of jail the prior month. God does not play favorites; He will mend your brokenness if you are willing. The broken look like you and me. The broken are educated, rich, poor, sick, healthy, and beautiful. It is time every christian leader awakens their spiritual senses and move forward with the kingdom work they have been called to do.

One of the most excellent recipes for self-respect is your relationship with Jesus and the discipline to hear His voice. Priorities distract us from our relationship with God. However, to grow stronger in the spirit, we must surrender to God first each day. Unfortunately, the flesh wrestles with us each day to put itself first. In Jesus, we are redeemed, and discipline enables us to resist temptation. Seek Him even when you do not feel like it. You will not regret spending your time with Him. The Holy Spirit helps us against the distraction of the world. You have all the energy you need. The key is to invest your energy in a healthier you intentionally.

It is up to you to choose God and invite Christ to transform you spiritually. Through Him, you can achieve self-respect, but most importantly, receive the power of the Holy Spirit.

The song "Beautiful" by Neryah Simeon is the perfect reminder of who you are.

Look how beautiful you are
Look at your beauty
Look what God created; He created you
The one and only you
Look at you
You are perfectly beautiful as you
God is within you; you will not fail
His light shines through you
Look how strong you are
Look how far you've come
It's time to rise, it's time to show the world who you are
With Jesus, you can do it all
Look how beautiful you are
Look at your beauty
Look what God created; He created you
The one and only you
Look at you
You are perfectly beautiful
You are perfectly beautiful as you
He created you
He made you who you are
He created you
The one and only you
Look at you
You are perfectly beautiful
You are perfectly beautiful as you.

CHAPTER 5

ACHIEVE

"You may delay, but time will not, and lost time is never found again."

~ Benjamin Franklin

No one starts out wanting to fail their goal. We set goals and naturally want to feel like we are growing. We measure ourselves based on short-term to long-term goals—yearly, quarterly, monthly, and weekly objectives determine our accomplishments. In the workplace or at home, regardless of how you measure them, crushing the objective is the goal, and recognition is the incentive. However, it demands physical, mental, emotional, and spiritual strength to achieve high performance.

GO AHEAD, CELEBRATE YOUR ACHIEVEMENTS

Compliments are a proven tool for reframing our self-limiting beliefs. Yet, we have a hard time accepting praise. Most times because we do not want to seem like we are bragging. Stating facts is not bragging. If you are like me, compliments make you feel uncomfortable. Practice saying "thank you" and nothing else. The hardest part about saying thank you will be not adding a diminishing comment about yourself.

Studies show that giving yourself credit for what you have accomplished, big or small, regardless of whether no one else recognizes you, sends positive brain feelings that motivate you to achieve more. When you compliment yourself for finishing a project, losing one pound, cooking a great dinner, graduating college, nailing a big presentation, or walking out of a toxic relationship, your brain can remember and repeat that skill. This process in your brain helps you take a step forward towards your achievements. Dr. Teresa Amabile, a professor at Harvard Business school, states, "Even if you're bad at taking a compliment, or you're not getting external recognition, you can still enjoy major psychological benefits from celebrating your achievements on your own."

If you haven't celebrated your accomplishment today, I invite you to honor and celebrate your achievements. Take a few minutes and write your accomplishments daily; it will transform your productivity. Most importantly, celebrate them; you have accomplished more than you give yourself credit.

Complement yourself, do not wait for others to recognize your achievements. Your future self will thank you.

STAY IN THE GAME

You cannot win a game you do not play, but you can lose by not playing. Do you fear the future? Are you living life, or are you letting life slip through your fingers because you are afraid to live? A normal instinct when one experiences fear is to run away, freeze or do nothing. While fear has a place in our lives, it also plays a role in how we live out our life. Let's face it, fear is normal, and it will always be there, but to live a life of no regrets, we must face our fears. Easier said than done, right?

IN REAL LIFE: WE CAN OVERCOME FEAR

Walking through the fear zone is part of the growth process. I was never a runner and one day decided to take up running. I could barely walk a mile the first few weeks. Every week I kept walking until my body just started running one day. Excited about my progress, I signed up for a half-marathon. I followed a training plan, and I was ready. I do not listen to music when I run because I like to be aware of my surroundings. I chat with God during my runs. It makes my runs go fast, and we get to catch up on a lot. He knew my fears and, over and over again through my runs, showed me I could make it. The day came, and I talked myself out of it. I made up every excuse in the book until I made myself believe I was not ready, and it was better not to make a fool out of myself. Truth be told, I cried because I could not believe it; I let myself down. The fear of failure stopped me in my tracks.

I was not racing for first place; I was running for fun, and still, fear managed to win. I stopped running and gave it up. Mostly because that was my time with God, and I knew I would need to have the conversation with Him at some point. I know pretty silly of me to limit God only to my running time. Later that year, I became pregnant, and eight weeks later, I had a miscarriage. It was not enough to feel like a failure for letting fear consume me, but now I'm thinking my body is not working. Wrong! There are numerous reasons why the body may miscarry. Thankfully, I began to run and found comfort and joy in running again. I signed up to run another half marathon later that year. This time, determined not to let fear stop me, I found an accountability partner to ensure I would not back down. I ran the whole race, and I felt like a million dollars.

One week after the race, I found out I was seven-weeks pregnant. Our beautiful and healthy baby girl ran that race with me in my belly, to my surprise. I continued to jog and walk throughout my pregnancy; it kept us healthy. I remember thinking, what if I had made it to the first race? Would my first pregnancy have turned out different? I would never know, but one thing I know for a fact is I finished a half marathon at 39 years old while pregnant and gave birth to a beautiful warrior princess. Take that fear!

If overcoming failure is possible, then our biggest defeat is submitting to fear. "Fear of failure may be construed as a self-evaluative framework that influences how the individual defines, orients to, and experiences failure in achievement situations."[110] Studies confirm most of us think of failure as an intolerable event.[111] We see failure as a negative implication of our self-worth and personal security, leading us to avoid disappointment proactively. Many of us will sabotage ourselves and avoid attending a networking event because of fear of rejection. Unfortunately, intentionally avoiding putting yourself in situations where you could fail will keep you from where you are

---

[110] McGregor, H.A., & Elliot, A.J. (2005). The shame of failure: Examining the link between fear of failure and shame. *Personality & Social Psychology Bulletin, 31*(2), 218-231.
[111] McGregor, H.A., & Elliot, A.J. (2005). The shame of failure: Examining the link between fear of failure and shame. *Personality & Social Psychology Bulletin, 31*(2), 218-231.

meant to shine. This mindset keeps us from achieving our biggest dreams. Imagine the missed possibilities; your biggest sponsor could be at the event ready to invest in someone like you.

PRACTICAL EXERCISE

It is time you own the things you can control. It is time to challenge your fears.

- Can you think of a time when your self-confidence was down and excuses easily poured out?
- What are the masks you are wearing to keep yourself from being fully known?
    1. Be honest in your answer, take your time, do not rush; it will take time to open up.

- What will happen if you sit idle in your fear?

- List your top three strengths.
1. _____
2. _____
3. _____

- How are you leveraging your strengths daily? Weekly? Monthly? If you are not leveraging your strengths, identify a project at work, in the community, at church, or at home where you can use your talents.
- When was the last time you did something courageous? Courage is not always flashy. Remember, courage sometimes means having the courage to try again tomorrow.

- What is one thing you wish you could have the courage to do?
  2. What is the consequence of not doing this?
  3. What is the best thing that can happen if you move forward?
- Now, close your eyes and imagine the possibilities, if fear was not an option.
- Where did your imagination take you?
  4. Did you renew old friendships, apologize, start a family, start your book, share your talents, inspire a nation, finish your education, buy a new home, ask for a promotion, go on a vacation across the world?
- What courageous step can you take today?

IN REAL LIFE: YOU ARE RESTORED

Wanda always dreamed of the perfect family, and in a rush to have it all, she married young. However, the abuse from her husband and her life experiences had convinced her she did not need a family. In an effort to leave her toxic marriage and fear of raising a child on her own, Wanda decided to stop the beating heart of the child she was carrying; she chose to have an abortion. Wanda accepted her fears as the norm and refused to fight to achieve her dream. The sorrow that hunted her pushed Wanda to scripture, and slowly she began to know her creator. Her relationship with Christ liberated Wanda from the fear holding her back. Wanda decided to follow her dreams and obtain a degree. She graduated from college and was hired in corporate America—her dream job shortly after.

Wanda's decision to get an abortion still haunts her many years later. She never had children of her own. Wanda's relationship with God restored her, and God's forgiveness has given her confidence she will meet her child in heaven one day. Mother's Day no longer brings her shame; it gives her hope and peace. Wanda found love in her late 50s that came with grandchildren from her marriage. With a big smile, she told me how much she loves the grandchildren and how they lovingly call her "Mima Wanda." Wanda's story brings hope to the broken and strength to the weak. God knows the desires of your heart; all you have to do is let Him in and allow Him to transform your life. God can restore you, too. We all have a story where fear has taken control of our actions. Know you are forgiven.

The COVID-19 pandemic has created a new level of fear in people. A fear that became impossible to deny. Loved ones are dying due to the effects of COVID-19. Others are dying of depression from being sheltered from those they love. Fear is real, and so is growth. Taking the appropriate precautions is critical—not only during a pandemic but in general. No one is advocating to go full throttle without safety. It takes time to prepare for a race as a runner, but it all starts with taking one step forward. It begins with exploring and pivoting to reach your goals differently. The goal is to take one action forward against the headwinds—challenge your fears, and you will see yourself soar.

PRACTICAL EXERCISE

Facing your fears is not easy, but not facing them weakens your power and puts your future at risk. Fear is like a computer virus. When a computer virus takes over, it can destroy your processor.

To prevent a virus, you must be proactive. Consider these steps to guard yourself against fear.

- **Identify and list your fears.** All fears, no matter how big or small. If you can't pinpoint a fear. Think about opportunities you avoid or dreams you have not conquered. Find the theme, and you will be able to identify the fear.
- **Confession.** Confess your worries to God.
- **Avoid perfectionism.** Perfectionism often leads to procrastination.
- **Invite change in your life.** Start small, eat something different, try a different workout routine, or even take a new route home.
- **Define yourself.** Remind yourself failure does not define you.
- **Stop comparing yourself to others.** Your journey is your own and irrelevant to where anyone else is in their journey.
- **Be aware of how you speak to yourself.** The tongue has the power of life and death, and those who love it will eat its fruit.
- **Take baby steps.** God knows His plan for you, and often the whole picture can seem unattainable and scary. Stop worrying so much about where you will be 10 years from now and focus more on what you can control—your day-to-day habits and mindset. Before you know it, fear no longer will hold you hostage. It may be present, but it will not paralyze you, allowing you to reach in five years what you thought you could not even accomplish in 10.

- **Be brave enough to need people.** Vulnerability is often viewed as weakness, but being vulnerable makes you bold. Find a friend to share your enjoyment and share your troubles with. If you fall, your friend can help you up. But if you fall without having a friend nearby, it will be harder to get up. Not impossible, but yes, a little more challenging.
- **Find a mentor.** Proverbs 13:20 reminds us, "Walk with the wise and become wise, for a companion of fools suffers harm."

SPIRITUAL CONNECTION

Do not allow your fears to get in the way of your success. Fear holds us back; it torments and hinders us. We grow through failure; consider being afraid not to fail. Fear of failure correlates with self-shaming and a fixed mindset. The key to overcoming fear is to confess your worries to God, including unconscious fears. Fears have to yield to the Holy Spirit. God is the prince of peace, and we are in a relationship with Him; peace conquers all. Do not discount God's voice. Remember you are in control, tell fear to get behind you, and take action, march forward. There will always be disapproval, even when you do everything right. It's time you face your fears head-on and take back your life; God did not create you to live in fear. Remember, you only need God's approval to achieve your highest potential. Nothing will give you more peace than fulfilling your purpose.

SELF-SABOTAGE

Have you ever wanted something really badly and realized you were the only person in the way of achieving it? People often sabotage themselves consciously and unconsciously through actions to disrupt their success. Many times, your actions impede you from fulfilling your personal and professional dreams. From believing you are not worthy to unconsciously hurting those around you, self-sabotage results in destructive self-behavior. Some people go as far as to alter their dreams to support the self-limiting thoughts holding them back.

Self-sabotage shows up in different forms. Experiences, habits, and thoughts influence our behavior and societal norms; these experiences or beliefs often influence our reasoning. People who self-sabotage often take action and fabricate beliefs and desires to make their behavior rational.[112] Self-sabotagers habitually alter their views to support the fictional theories.[113] Self-sabotage will often have us blaming others, the environment, our past or current situation for supporting the actions that take us off track from achieving our goals. Common signs of self-sabotage include but are not limited to delaying important commitments, creating a negative narrative about yourself, setting objectives with no action plan, not trying, and lack of self-control.

IN REAL LIFE: WE CAN FIND OUR WORTH

At 16 years of age, Marina married and, soon after, they welcomed home a healthy child. When the child was born, she loved her child dearly, yet she felt hopeless, lost, and could not

---

[112] D'Cruz, J. (2020). Rationalization and self-sabotage. Behavioral and Brain Sciences, 43.
[113] D'Cruz, J. (2020). Rationalization and self-sabotage. Behavioral and Brain Sciences, 43.

keep up with school and the baby. She decided to quit high school and dedicate herself to raising her child and future children. Her relationship with her husband kept turning for the worse. He was abusive, and although she wanted a better life for her and her three children, she continued to self-sabotage by procrastinating her next move. She convinced herself she needed her husband to make it in the world with the three children. She self-sabotaged herself, creating a sad story of herself. She told herself that she could not get a decent job without an education. She also had convinced herself it would be difficult for her to go to school with three kids. Finally, she even believed the abuse was not as bad since she was still strong enough to care for what mattered most to her—the children.

One day he gave her permission to get a job at a supermarket; he said the additional money would help the growing family. Without hesitation, she agreed, and it changed her life. People recognized her for her capabilities, and slowly, she realized her worth. Although she did not know she was sabotaging her life at the time, the community at work helped her see her potential. In time, she walked away from the abusive relationship and successfully cared for her children. However, she did not stop there. Once she realized her worth, excuses did not exist in her vocabulary. Her life would be very different today if she did not know her self-worth. Realizing her self-worth pushed her further than she could ever imagine. Marina went back to school and now holds an MBA and is a successful leader in a well-known organization.

Everything in life is temporary. One must be careful not to allow the present circumstances to dictate the future. Marina realized there was more to life than raising children in an abusive relationship. She realized she had everything she needed inside of her to own her narrative. She grew into a powerhouse, single-handly raised her three children, obtained an education, and landed her dream job. Marina is confident God opened the doors for her to meet a community of women that opened her eyes to the greatness God had already put in her.

PRACTICAL EXERCISE

- Take a moment and write down the top three things you continue to postpone in your life. Yes, right now, this moment, write them down.

1. _____

2. _____

3. _____

- Next, answer why you have not prioritized these items.
- Next, systematically ask yourself why multiple times and document the response until uncovering the root cause. Understanding the root cause will enable you to concentrate on the right strategy to move forward. Let's take a look at this example.

Example: I continue to delay making the appointment to complete my yearly physical.

1. Why? I have been busy with work and life.
2. Why? I do not have time for myself.
3. Why? I know what the doctor is going to say.

4. Why? I do not make myself a priority.

5. I do not want the additional responsibility of the changes required to achieve a healthier me.

The goal here is to continue to ask yourself why until you get to the root cause. In this case, it is apparent self-sabotage.

SPIRITUAL CONNECTION

In Scripture, Moses narrates the story of Jacob and Esau. Esau was the eldest son and the rightful heir of his father. One day Esau came home late from working in the fields and was starved and tired. His younger brother had finished cooking a wonderful and savory stew. Esau asked his brother Jacob to let him eat some of his stew. However, Jacob told him only if he gave up his birthright. Esau's temporary need to satisfy his hunger drove him to sabotage his future for a bowl of stew. Esau could have cooked food for himself or grabbed fruit from the field as a snack until he could regain the strength to cook his dinner. Yet, he chose to give up his rightful birthright. Are you sabotaging your future to feed a temporary need? It is common for one to discard their well-being for a quick high. A temporary condition could be the need for company, resources, or indulging in food to satisfy the stress. The momentary joy that destroys you long-term can come in the ways of sex, food, toxic relationships, alcohol, drugs, self-sabotage, and others. In all cases, all can ultimately destroy you and those you love.

COURAGEOUS LEADERSHIP

Meaning gives purpose and significance. Research suggests

meaning in life supersedes life satisfaction.[114] Unfortunately, many of us spend our energy busy with meaningless things and dedicate little time to finding meaning.[115] Leaders assess how meaningful their work is and how it contributes to the organization's vision in the workplace. Yet, spend little time on what sparks meaning in us.

Is your career your calling, or is your purpose more significant than your career? As individuals, we limit our imagination and mute our purpose, making it difficult to find meaning. What do you value? Does your environment manifest joy, or does it suppress your sense of life? Understanding your purpose and clarifying your why is essential because your why will inspire you during difficult times and build resilience to accomplish your goals. The same way an organization's culture can silence or enable innovation, your environment can suppress your purpose.

SPIRITUAL CONNECTION

My why has changed over the years, but creating what I want to see has always been my gift. Growing up escaping poverty gave me the courage to push past my fears. Now that I have a family and a career, my family is my why, and for them, I courageously face the world each day to fulfill my purpose. Some days I fail miserably; other days, I breathe victory. But I know one thing, giving up is not an option. My why is my family and my confidence is in Jesus.

Once you understand your purpose and find meaning in

[114] Steger, M.F., Frazier, P., Oishi, S. & Kaler, M. (2006). The meaning in life questionnaire: Assessing the presence of and search for meaning in life. *Journal of Counseling Psychology*, 53(I), 80—93.

[115] Schwartz, T. & Loehr, J. (2003). *The Power of Full Engagement: Managing Energy, Not Time, is the Key to High Performance and Personal Renewal.* United States: Free Press.

life, your actions must support your goals to reach your vision. We are reminded in 2 Timothy 1:7, "For the Spirit God gave us does not make us timid, but gives us power, love, and self-discipline." In the book of Esther 8, we learn about Esther. She is an admirable woman who courageously follows through with her purpose despite the fear and potential negative consequences she would face. Esther recognized her meaning in life was taking a stand, bringing change, and saving the Jews. King Ahasuerus had given a decree to end the life of all Jews. During Esther's time, no one was permitted in the king's company unless asked to the king's presence. Esther's meaning in life superseded her satisfaction to live in King Ahasuerus' home, and she found the courage to speak up for what was morally right. Esther's bravery saved the Jews.

Mary Magdalene was an afflicted woman and enslaved person to the demons that consumed her mind and well-being. Jesus healed Mary of the evil spirits troubling her and her infirmities. Mary could have let her past ruin her future. People probably judged her past, but it did not stop Mary. Instead, Mary's grit and courage had been silenced by the enemy no more, and she courageously moved forward. Mary became a disciple of Jesus and one of the most prominent females in scripture.

Are you operating in courageous leadership? Courage is about stepping forward in faith. It is about understanding what is in front of you and taking action on what no one else sees. Courageous leaders move forward despite fear and take the right actions to achieve results. Brave leaders will step up during difficult and uncertain times. People can develop over time into courageous leaders with proper development and efforts.

However, they must be willing to step out of their comfort zone to positively impact their lives and others' lives.[116]

Your attitude is essential when it comes to courageous leadership. In fact, your attitude is more important than your intelligence. Psychologist Albert Bandura once said, "If you think you can, you probably can. If you think you can't—well, that self-limiting and self-fulfilling belief might well stop you from doing something you are perfectly capable of doing." Doubting yourself can cost your dream career, mental peace, your family, joy, and your dreams.

Dr. Martin Luther King Jr. rose against the norm and stood up for freedom. Sadly, discrimination is still alive and well in the United States today. Many of us today carry painful mental and physical racism wounds. Imagine how much more difficult it was for Dr. King to stand up for what he believed during his time. Dr. King exemplifies courageous leadership at its best. His work was cut short. However, his bold leadership lives on and reminds us to be fearless about moral things in life. Matthew 5:13-16 reminds us that "we are salt of the earth" and the "light of the world." To be a courageous leader and achieve your most significant potential, you must be ready to shine a light on the darkest areas of your life. It is easier to call out the darkness in others, but you must face the darkness in your life to be great. To leave a footprint in the world, you must take a step forward. It is not easy to stare fear in the eye and do the right thing. However, with God, all things are possible.

Some would argue courageous leadership is not linked to power and control. Courageous leadership does not always

---

[116] Phillips, J.J. & Phillips, P. P. (2020). Courageous leadership: Delivering results in turbulent times. *Strategic HR Review,* 19(2), 59-66. doi:10.1108/SHR-01-2020-0002.

show up in a title, power, and authority.[117] A fearless leader often steps up in a time of trouble, calls out unethical actions, writes that book, says no, walks away from the toxic relationship, takes the less traveled road, and is not afraid to grow. "Every worthwhile accomplishment has a price tag in terms of hard work, patience, faith, and endurance."[118] Courageous leadership helps you through tough times. The most impactful leaders are vulnerable; they do not always have all the answers and are not afraid to admit it. Vulnerability is not a one-time event. Being vulnerable with your experiences is essential to stay open to learning, new experiences, and most importantly, to achieve long-term success.[119] It takes great courage to acknowledge you are not perfect.[120] The reality is no one is perfect. To achieve success, being open and transparent about the opportunities is critical.[121] The pressures society imposes on people to be perfect can drain you. The key is to surround yourself with ethical, intelligent, humble people who believe in your vision. Leaders can influence at any level. Whether you realize it or not, you positively or negatively impact others around you.

Regardless of your title, you can inspire others. A student can inspire other students, a woman can inspire a community, and a teammate can inspire a whole team. When you are open about

[117] Chapman, M. (2020). Courageous leadership — What defines it in the modern organisation. *Strategic HR Review*, 19(2), 47-50. doi:10.1108/SHR-01-2020-0001.
[118] Engstrom, T.W. (1976). *The Making of a Christian Leader: How to Develop Management and Human Resources Skills*, Grand Rapids, MI: Zondervan.
[119] Van Velsor, E.V., McCauley, C.D., & Ruderman, M.N. (Eds.), 2010. *The Center for Creative Leadership Handbook of Leadership Development* (3rd Ed.) San Francisco, CA. Jossey-Bass.
[120] Chapman, M. (2020). Courageous leadership — what defines it in the modern organisation. *Strategic HR Review*, 19(2), 47-50. doi:10.1108/SHR-01-2020-0001.
[121] Hlupic, V. (2020). Courageous leadership: Anita Krohn Traaseth, former CEO of Innovation Norway. *Strategic HR Review*, 19(2), 51-54. doi:10.1108/SHR-11-2019-0082.

tho aroac you struggle with yet, do not use them as an excuse to keep you from achieving your goals. Your resiliency inspires those around you. If you continually walk away because things get complicated, you will inspire those around you to quit as well. The reality is everyone will struggle at one point or another. However, no one should feel like they are the only one.

THE IMPOSTER PHENOMENON

Dr. Pauline Clance and Suzanne Imes introduced the term "imposter phenomenon" in the late 1970s, more widely known today as imposter syndrome. Imposter syndrome refers to individuals who feel they are a fraud even though they are intelligent people.[122] Imposter syndrome is a blocker to our achievements. It is estimated 7 out of 10 of us will experience imposter syndrome at least once in our lives.[123] Imposter syndrome convinces you that you do not belong. "The clinical symptoms most frequently reported are generalized anxiety, lack of self-confidence, depression, and frustration related to the inability to meet self-imposed standards of achievement."[124]

Impostors exhibit an extremely high standard of perfectionism, low self-confidence, and behaviors that hinder their growth.[125] Other common signs of imposter syndrome include self-sabotage, fear, self-doubt, and creating negative criticism

[122] Clance, P.R., & Imes, S.A. (1978). The imposter phenomenon in high achieving women: Dynamics and therapeutic intervention. *Psychotherapy: Theory, Research & Practice*, 15(3), 241–247.
[123] Sakulku, J. (I). The Impostor Phenomenon. The Journal of Behavioral Science, 6(I), 75-97.
[124] Clance, P.R., & Imes, S.A. (1978). The imposter phenomenon in high achieving women: Dynamics and therapeutic intervention. *Psychotherapy: Theory, Research & Practice*, 15(3), 241–247.
[125] Badawy, R.L., Gazdag, B.A., Bentley, J.R. & Brouer, R. L. (2018). Are all impostors created equal? Exploring gender differences in the impostor phenomenon-performance link. *Personality and Individual Differences*, 131, 156-163.

about your performance. Unfortunately, some experts will never believe they are smart enough. Many of us will experience burnout because we think we must work harder, or someone will find out we are not smart enough. The good news is you can overcome imposter syndrome.

IN REAL LIFE: WE CAN BEAR FRUIT AMID THE STORM

She was offered the chief executive officer position for a rapidly growing organization. Her mentors and sponsors reassured her of her ability to succeed, and she did. However, 25-plus years of stellar performance and promotion after promotion did not stop her from feeling she somehow had fooled everyone. Tasha said, "Every day I felt that was the day my luck would run out, and everyone would know I'm not as smart as they think." Overcoming imposter syndrome is absolutely possible, but it is not easy. We must continuously balance overworking and being more practical to prove that we are not a fraud and are competent to lead. It takes courage to believe you are intelligent, and you earned every right to sit at the table. Daily affirmations are promising interventions to begin the process of nourishing the smart and strong woman inside of you. As you can see, achieving success does not mean you have activated your power.

One of the most powerful tools accessible to us at all times is the power to pause. Pausing and taking a deep breath can help you connect with yourself to assess your thoughts, emotions, and beliefs.[126] When you leverage the power of pause, you are

---

[126] Theodores, D. (2020). The 3 C's of courageous leadership: How to connect to your body, connect to your creativity, connect to your inner revolutionary. *Strategic HR Review*, 19(2), 81-83.

more effective at the actions you take. You also are more capable of taking a calculated risk and stepping out of your comfort zone. Go ahead, be courageous, take a deep breath, pause for a minute, remember who you are—you. You belong in that job. You belong at that table. You are made for a time like this.

SPIRITUAL CONNECTION

During a storm or dry season, as long as the branches stay attached to the tree, the branch can bear fruit again. A branch not anchored on the tree will dry and die because it cannot receive nutrients. When we are far from God, we cannot receive the nourishment needed to strengthen us during difficult times.

God says in John 15, "I am the true vine, and My Father is the vinedresser. Every branch in Me that does not bear fruit He takes away; and every branch that bears fruit He prunes, that it may bear more fruit. You are already clean because of the word I have spoken to you. Abide in Me, and I in you. As the branch cannot bear fruit of itself, unless it abides in the vine, neither can you, unless you abide in Me." To abide in a place, we must first understand where we are standing.

Some of us want the fairytale but give up the minute things do not go according to plan. There are different sources to get your nutrients to achieve your goals, but they will not be sustainable. Jesus warns us that there are other sources where we will be malnourished and separate us from Christ. God provides the living water, peace, and strength during difficult times. The world offers materialistic things, jobs, awards, and recognition, but all cannot give you peace.

However, when you know Jesus, the world cannot deceive you.

We are called to bear fruit in our purpose. Just like the vinedresser cares for and cultivates the vine to enjoy the fruits, you also must care for yourself and nourish yourself in Christ. The branches grow because it is receiving nutrients from the vine. What is your source of power? Your source of power matters. More than ever, the world needs leaders guided by the Holy Spirit.

IN REAL LIFE: FAITH WILL SEE YOU THROUGH THE DARKEST TIMES

Anna grew up in a broken home with an abusive stepfather. At 18, she graduated high school and decided to leave home and start a new life. She moved to a different state and began to attend college. The future was promising, but the process was painful. Although Anna wanted to change, her fears dominated her emotions and actions. Her fear of failure was too great to withstand the transformation process, and she returned to what she knew. The abusive environment was safer than transforming her life to achieve her best self. Anna gave up on her dream to become a doctor. What she once hated—chaos, dishonor, pain, and anxiety, had somehow become what she desired.

Mary Anne Radmacher is a writer and artist who once said, "Courage doesn't always roar. Sometimes courage is the quiet voice at the end of the day saying, 'I will try again tomorrow.'" Anna's most outstanding achievement was trying each day again to leave the cave of fear holding her back, and that is OK. Anna may not be leaping, but she is putting one foot forward each day, and as long as she dares to keep going, she will make it. Anna may not become a doctor, or maybe she will, but I am confident she will find her purpose because I believe God will complete the work He began in her.

Dara lived in misery and pain for most of her life. The things she experienced—most of us would be unable to endure. Dara was no stranger to deception and the victim of others' sins. At age 10, alcohol became her source of strength until it was not. You see, at age 3, Dara was separated from her parents. At age 7, the United States government rescued her from child traffickers. Filled with the hope of seeing her parents again, Dara was ready to be reunited with her parents.

Under supervision from family court, Dara was reunited with her mother in a small room. The court representative stepped away to give them privacy. When the representative returned, she found what you would only see in horror movies. There was blood everywhere. Dara's mother stabbed her 17 times and left her to die. Miraculously, Dara survived, and one year later, her birth mother was sentenced to life in prison. The sad truth is, Dara's mother had sold her to child traffickers, and finding her had consequences. Dara was placed once again in a foster home. In the foster home, she was sexually abused and beaten. To escape the pain, Dara became addicted to alcohol. At age 13, the alcohol was not enough to calm the horror, and Dara attempted suicide.

Once again, Dara survived the sins of others. This time she was placed in a foster home where she found a loving father figure. Although the family treated her well, Dara continued drinking. Sadly, her foster father passed away 10 years later. When she lost the only person who showed her love, her foster dad, alcohol became even more pronounced. At age 27, her liver failed, and she was hospitalized. Now a single mother on the verge of dying, Dara found hope in Jesus Christ. Now that

Dara abides in God, she has renewed strength. Dara forgave her mother (her mother died in prison, and Dara never saw her again). Today, Dara has an excellent job, is finishing her college degree, writing a book about her life, is raising a healthy young boy, and in 2020 purchased her first home. Perseverance is the great enemy of defeat. Dara faces challenges each day, but she has peace, hope, and determination to rise above her past and build a better future for her and her child.

There is a clear difference between Anna and Dara's stories. Dara's faith is more significant than her fear despite the painful past. Anna's faith is in her ability alone. She has the opportunity to break off the chains of fear and complete her transformation. Unfortunately, no one can do it alone. Thankfully, the Holy Spirit dwells in us and we are never alone. The transformations are never comfortable, but the end will always be better than where you started.

TALENTS

God assigned talents to every person and empowered us to use our gifts. Your talent is valuable to those around you; it is not to be taken for granted. A Gallup workplace study shows that employees who leverage their talents consistently outperform those who do not.[127] People who use their strengths also are more happy, productive, and less likely to quit their jobs. Unfortunately, most people undervalue what they inherently do well. People often focus on their weaknesses instead of developing their strengths. Sadly, if you do not value your strengths, you will spend your life trying to be someone you are

---

[127] Flade, P., Asplund, J., & Elliot, G. (2015). Employees who use their strengths outperform those who don't. *Gallup News*.

not. Do not delegate your gifts to someone else. Your talents were placed in you by the most excellent author of life; your gift will change lives.

IN REAL LIFE: OUR TALENTS ARE MEANT TO SHINE

I have always loved to teach, inspire, and empower women. Shining the light on the success of other women gives me joy. Fear of speaking in public because of my accent kept my talent hidden from the world for years. Yet, my ability to connect with women at every level was a shining strength. Opportunities to speak would surface, and I gladly recommended other speakers until I was told, "No, we want you." Although I was extremely nervous, I accepted. To my surprise, I inspired the audience— the line of women who wanted to speak to me after the speech ran over an hour. My talent outshined my fear of speaking. I was the answer the audience needed to hear that day.

I continued to take on speaking engagements, the more I sharpen my strengths the more confident and impactful I became. I was no longer a public speaker; I am now a global inspirational speaker. Public speaking was not my weakness; I only needed to sharpen my strengths. Connecting and inspiring a room brings me joy and purpose.

We each have a unique talent. For some of us, connecting and supporting others is a talent that helps others achieve their dreams. I call it the dream enabler. Writing the perfect speech or song that will inspire others is a perfect example of leveraging your talent to help others achieve their best performance. However, we spend so much time working on our weaknesses, we forget to grow our divine talents. We lose the joy in what we love and silence our strength and the impact to transform others.

SPIRITUAL CONNECTION

In the parable of talents in Matthew 25:14, the master gives five talents to one servant, two to another, and one to the third. Scripture states the first two servants used and multiplied their talents. Yes, the more you use your talents, the more God multiplies. However, the last servant was afraid and hid his talent. God created every one of us with a purpose; our talents are for His glory. Each time we hide our talents, we are dishonoring our creator. Your achievements or lack of actions will influence others positively or negatively. It is not too late to activate your talent and be the light you are meant to be.

As leaders, modeling the way is one of the most effective ways to inspire others to use their talents.[128] No matter how fancy it is, verbal communication means nothing unless the leader models the behavior he expects from others. Michael Jordan is one of the most incredible players ever known to basketball. Jordan did not let anything get in the way of sharpening his strengths and achieving greatness. Jordan's failure to make it in the high school tryouts did not rob him of his dream. Instead, it gave him the courage to try harder, making him stronger; he used it as an opportunity for growth. Jordan modeled the way inside and outside the court. He gave his best inside and outside the court. Jordan practiced diligently to continue to improve his game and perfect his strengths. Jordan did not only achieve his dream to play in the National Basketball Association; he is one of the greatest basketball players of all time. Jordan's action encourages people who have not perfected their strength and gives them hope to achieve their dreams.

---

[128] Kouzes, J.M., & Posner, B.Z. (2007). *The leadership Challenge,* 6th edition, San Francisco, CA: Jossey-Bass.

Keep in mind not everyone will see the potential in you. Not everyone will recognize the raw talent that only needs practice and nourishment. People will quickly discount you, just like they discounted Jordan. Do not quit; grow your strength, and you will find your purpose will give you the power to achieve your accomplishments. Most importantly, it will empower you to walk in your purpose with strength, authority, and peace.

Rose was only 15 when she made the courageous decision she would break the generational cycle of dropping out of high school. Her family lived paycheck to paycheck, and her ability to work at 15 would bring income to the home. She decided she did not need to quit school to work. Every day, she went to school, worked after school, late nights, and weekends. It was challenging to study while working. But she realized if she did not lead by example, her younger siblings would never know quitting was not the only option. Her older siblings and family members did not recognize her talent to plan her day and maximize each hour to succeed strategically. Instead, she was made fun of and rejected.

One day her mother whispered in her ear, "I'm proud of you. I see you; keep going, baby girl." No other words were spoken, but it was all she needed to feed her strength. Rose went on to graduate college and opened a family business. Her younger siblings followed in her footsteps and became successful, and her older siblings now own part of the family company. Today, their family business is thriving, and her mother and dad are enjoying their early retirement.

Rose modeled the way at an early age for the whole family. She did not have role models in her family. Yet, Rose was determined to become a role model for the family. Her determination to change her family's history enabled her to model the way, impact the future, and give onlookers hope. She used her imagination to create a vision worth fighting for and took action each day, moved forward and fulfilled her dream.

Not everyone will recognize your worth; do not let that someone be you. We are reminded in 1 Timothy 4:12, "Don't let anyone look down on you because you are young, but set an example for the believers in speech, in conduct, in love, in faith, and purity." If God calls you to lead, trust He has planted the talent you need to achieve change and transformation. Do not fear the lack of education and experience. Fear not using your skills today to bring positive change to your future and those you love the most.

WRITE YOUR VISION

Organizations build strategies to bring their visions to life and invest time in creating strategies to anticipate the actualized objectives. It is time you make an action plan to realize your vision, to bring to life the best version of you.

King Solomon wrote in Proverbs 29:18, "Where there is no vision, the people perish." This statement is true for all of us. A leader does not only imagine but takes action toward the vision, learning along the journey. Habbakuk 2 says, "Write the vision and make it plain." Having a vision for your life is an essential component of leading your life. Every successful person starts with the imagination of what they want to achieve. Our accomplishments are the fruit of our imagination. Writing your vision serves multiple purposes, but most importantly, it serves as your North Star. It allows you to prioritize your actions. A vision statement also helps us identify the change that must take place to achieve the future state. Our vision will help us stay focused on what really matters.

Understanding the direction in which you want to go is critical. If we do not know where we are going, our actions will become activities with no meaning. Chasing the wind is exhausting and can make you feel lost. It is up to you to take the steps needed to achieve your dreams. We can remain victims of our circumstances, or we can be victorious. You have everything you need to accomplish all you want to be. However, you must have a plan. Without a plan, external pressures will become your priorities. Remember to partner with God and let him influence your vision. Surrendering to God first enables us to silence distractions that interfere with our goals.

A leader's strategy to achieve its vision should incorporate a plan for short and long-term headwinds and tailwinds. An idea without a plan is worthless. The action plan does not need to be perfect, but you need a plan. Yes, you will have to revise it throughout your journey. There will be times when your plans will go smoothly, and other times you may feel you will never reach the goal.[129] Know it is ok to shift your timeline.

I've become dependent on the navigation Global Positioning System (GPS) in my car every time I take a trip. Without hesitation, the GPS reroutes when the straight path to our destination is blocked or when I take a wrong turn. Learn to reroute, stay the course, endure, do not give up, and watch your dreams become a reality.

---

[129] Van Velsor, E.V., McCauley, C.D., & Ruderman, M.N. (Eds.), 2010. *The Center for Creative Leadership Handbook of Leadership Development* (3rd Ed.) San Francisco, CA. Jossey-Bass.

PRACTICAL EXERCISE

Take the time to write down the vision for your life thoughtfully. Visions are typically bold and often scary. If you can achieve your dreams in a year, you are probably not thinking bold enough. If your dream is easily attainable, it is not a bold vision. We challenge the status quo daily in our organizations. Do not settle in your personal life. The responsibility starts and ends with you. The most significant risk you face is feeling comfortable with your achievements. Achievements are outstanding, but the minute you stop working towards a better you, the minute your mindset runs idle, your performance will suffer, and your dreams will grow stale.

- Make your future a priority and schedule two 30 minute sessions. One should say "time to imagine" and the other "time to plan." Go ahead, take a look at your calendar and schedule the time now.
- Write down all the roles you currently have—for example, teacher, wife, mother, mentor, executive, etc.

To begin writing your vision, consider asking yourself the following questions.

- **Dream:** Set time aside to create, imagine and dream. Even if you are not a creative individual, you can build a creative brain.
  - Give yourself permission to take a walk and observe the beautiful creation.
  - o activate your creativity, challenge yourself to

hrainstorm about a problem you are trying to
solve or any topic. Ensure to reduce distractions
by setting your phone on silent during this time.
I do my best thinking when I take walks or take a
shower, anywhere I can be alone in my thoughts.

- What are your life aspirations for the roles you identified
  in the step above physically, mentally, emotionally, and
  spiritually?
- What do you consider your values to be?
- What do you consider your strengths to be?
- What would others say are your strengths? For this one,
  I would recommend asking the people around you. You
  may be pleasantly surprised by what they see as your
  strengths.
- What do you want your legacy to be as a mother,
  executive, mentor, etc.?
- What would you people to say at your funeral?
- What would the fruits of the spirit feel and look like to
  you?
- What energizes you?
- What are you most proud of?
- When do you have the most fun?
- What would you like to do more of?
- What assumptions about you do you want to leave
  behind?
- What brings you the most joy?

Take the time to reflect on your answers.

- Next, list the benefits of making your vision come to life. What would your world be like if you were living your dream? I encourage you to challenge your thoughts, unleash your imagination, and write a bold vision declaration for yourself.

Your vision statement is only the beginning. Once you have a vision statement, the next step is to set your goals and timelines for achieving short and long-term milestones. Write an action plan to achieve your goals. A vision without action will remain an idea.

- Next, ask yourself the following questions.
  - Are you committed to your vision?

It starts with you, your commitment matters. This is your vision; it does not matter how many people root for you. Your vision will not bear fruit if you do not believe in yourself. Once you are committed to your vision statement, you must resist the temptation to deviate from it. No matter what, it is your responsibility to show up and take a step forward toward your vision each day.

- What needs to happen to realize the vision?
  - Write down each goal and every step required to bring the concept to life under each plan. While some goals may have a shorter time frame, be clear on the actions' sequence or if specific steps must take simultaneously before moving on to the next step.

- What are the resources you need to achieve your vision? Resources may include time, finances, support with the children while in school or working, expertise, assets, and an additional pair of hands.
- Share your vision and consider who you should align with to support your vision?

When I decided to pursue my doctorate, I aligned with God, my husband, parents, and pastor. The pursuit of the doctorate needed to be in God's plans for my life. Obtaining a doctorate requires hard work, and I knew it would be impossible if not for God's purpose. I needed my husband's prayer, support, and alignment. I knew the next few years would not be easy, and knowing I had his blessing and alignment, and the school was now a priority, and was critical. I also needed my parents' alignment to support us in the care of our children. Their support would help ensure no one burned out, and we all remained focused. Finally, I needed prayer and support from our pastors. I cannot emphasize enough the importance of a support system. Having others support your vision will give you strength when you feel your dream seems too far to achieve.

There will be times when your support system may not help you due to unexpected circumstances. Make sure you also check up on your support system. The more aware you are, the easier it will be for you to pivot and engage others to support you.

One year, my mother ended up in the hospital for seven days. Our youngest son became ill with pneumonia and spent a few days in the hospital. Also, the workload from my job weighed heavy. Sleepless nights and long days made weeks a blur. My physical, mental, and spiritual well-being saved me from not breaking down. My body had been preparing for this type of stress and could tolerate it. However, let's be clear, my husband and I quickly worked on a plan to ensure we had the right support system around me. I could not have done it alone. I knew although I was physically, mentally, and spiritually healthy during that time, I needed intervals of rest and moments of prayer to recharge. This meant engaging the support system to allow me to sleep between three to four hours during those difficult days. My husband reminds me often, do not be a superhero; ask for help. Never sacrifice your physical, mental, emotional, and spiritual well-being for an extended period. Doing so will set you back more than you can imagine.

- How will you allocate the appropriate time to your vision?
- Understanding how you spend your time today is vital because you will need to deprioritize some things and prioritize others to achieve your vision.
- What will success look like for each objective?

Determining early on what success looks like will help you enjoy the small wins. It does not have to be perfect; a small win may mean staying on the journey until your next milestone.

There will be times when the weight of life may seem too heavy to carry; during those times, you want to lean heavier into your creator. When you align to God's vision for your life, He will see you through it.

While each step is integral to achieving your vision, without activation, nothing happens. It is now time to make it happen and implement the strategic plan to tackle the objectives needed to achieve your vision.

- Activate the Plan

A strategic plan activates the work toward your dream. It should include the daily actions required to realize the vision, how and when the activities will occur. If needed, adjust the plan while always focusing on the vision.

- Finally, evaluate your results, timeline, and method of execution often.

Vision boards are a common and powerful tool for creating a vision. Vision boards have proven to empower people to imagine the life they aspire to have.[130] Done right, your vision board should help you craft a plan and action steps to realize your vision. The most significant instrument needed to create a vision board is your imagination. Most people use a pinboard, scissors, tape, glue stick, and magazines to complete their vision board. You also can use technology to create a picture collage that you can print. The key is to put the vision into action to achieve your purpose.

Consistency is everything. Stay committed to your dream. If God gave you a vision, He would bring it to completion. God is the creator of life, and His plans for you are limitless. When we partner with God, we think differently. It is a different level of

---

[130] Burton, L., & Lent, J. (2016). The use of vision boards as a therapeutic intervention. *Journal of Creativity in Mental Health, 11*(1), 52-65.

thinking. Your vision may be challenging for others to understand when God is your partner. It is OK; it is God's vision for you, not them. Your accomplishments will be endless; while the journey will not be comfortable, you will have strength, peace, and joy. Remain disciplined to your vision—take action each day toward your goals. Ask yourself if how you are spending your time contributes to your goals. If it is not, it may be time to reassess your priorities. As you crush your objectives, be mindful not to let achievements and power make you prideful. A prideful person puts their needs first at the cost of others. While achieving your vision is transformational, it should never cause others pain. If it does, reassess your strategy. It may be that your plan needs to be adjusted versus giving up on your vision.

Pride fuels the quest for power and achievement. Studies have discovered two forms of pride—authentic and hubristic.[131] Authentic pride relates to feeling accomplished based on skills, self-esteem, advice-giving, and genuine success. Hubristic pride is linked to arrogance, dominance, intimation, and negative behaviors.[132]

SPIRITUAL CONNECTION

"Dominance is associated with traits such as narcissism, aggression, and disagreeableness."[133] In the quest for power and achievement, pride can make us believe we do not need

---

[131] Cheng, J.T., Tracy, J.L., & Henrich, J. (2010). Pride, personality, and the evolutionary foundations of human social status. *Evolution and Human Behavior*, *31*(5), 334-347.

[132] Cheng, J.T., Tracy, J.L., & Henrich, J. (2010). Pride, personality, and the evolutionary foundations of human social status. *Evolution and Human Behavior*, *31*(5), 334-347.

[133] Cheng, J.T., Tracy, J.L., & Henrich, J. (2010). Pride, personality, and the evolutionary foundations of human social status. *Evolution and Human Behavior*, *31*(5), 334-347.

God and lead us in the wrong direction. In Proverbs, King Solomon says, there are seven things the Lord despises, "A proud look (the attitude that makes one overestimate oneself and discount others), a lying tongue, hands that shed innocent blood, a heart that creates wicked plans, feet that run swiftly to evil, a false witness who breathes out lies (even half-truths), and one who spreads discord (rumors) among brothers."

Scripture reminds us the devil is the father of lies. Therefore, knowing God's voice is of absolute importance. If you do not know our Father's voice, satan may be whispering in your ear a vision that is not part of God's purpose for your life. Always make it a habit to bring your vision, goals, and plans before God. Remember, God is not a God of confusion. He is a God of peace, a God of order.

Is your life in order? Surrender yourself to Him today. Do not live another day in chaos and confusion. We must intentionally seek God's guidance each day and work towards a Christ-like character. Unfortunately, people have stopped pursuing a Christ-like character because they want to win their way.[134] Without God, the flesh will win every time; your achievements are limitless with God. Remember, Matthew 6:33 tells us to "Seek first the kingdom of God and His righteousness, and all these things shall be added to you."

Keeping our focus on Jesus Christ will enable us to conquer the flesh, activate our power, unlock our potential, and fulfill our purpose. Galatians reminds us, "For he who sows to his flesh will of the flesh reap corruption, but he who sows to the Spirit will of the spirit reap." Remember, all our triumphs start in our

---

[134] Lawson, D. (2008). Transforming Initiatives: Leadership ethics from the Sermon on the Mount. *The Journal of Applied Christian Leadership, 3*(1), 29-46.

minds. You have the power inside of you to succeed. Stand firm and know your worth; do not allow others to bully you with their limited imagination.

Lance Wubbels, the vice president of Literary Development at Koechel Peterson & Associates, once said, "From this moment forward... It is time to take action and unleash your best self! I stop the blame game and excuses. I am responsible for my life and for where I am today. I cannot blame the people and circumstances in my past, and I refuse to hide behind my past mistakes."

H.E.R.A.C.T.

Chapter 6

CONFIDENCE

"Confidence is contagious. So is lack of confidence."

~ Vince Lombardi

You do not have the right qualifications; we found someone more experienced than you. You will never find someone to love you. Your past is shameful; no one will want you on their team. You are a failure. You are not smart enough; you are a negative influence; your addiction will haunt you. You are too fat, too skinny, too bright, too weird. The words of leaders and loved ones echoed loud in my head each day until they became uncontrollable fuel. This fuel pushed me out of my comfort zone. I thought to myself, "Look at me now, an accomplished executive traveling the world, lacking nothing." Nothing worldly, that is, by society's standards, I was successful.

Sadly, the world could not see me deteriorating from the inside out. I lacked peace, love, self-worth, and genuine joy. My strength was admirable, but being vulnerable was out of the question. Anger, resentment, and bitterness darkened my heart with each passing day I had buried the harmful words so deep in my heart; I had forgotten them. But the painful words unconsciously birthed prevailing self-limiting beliefs. It did not matter what I achieved; it was never enough to quiet these confidence killers. Until one day, the thought of giving up and ending my life crossed my mind. The idea was so loud in my head it awakened my soul, and the resilient woman inside of me fought back one more time and screamed, "I'M HERE; THERE IS STILL HOPE. DO NOT GIVE UP." Desperately searching for answers, I remembered my because we do not want to seem like we are bragging. Stating facts is not bragging. If you are like me, compliments make you mother's words when she would hear me say I couldn't do something. "You are a child of God; you have the power to do anything through Him, seek Him," I screamed and cried out to God. I remember saying in between tears, "Holy Spirit intercede for me because my thoughts are controlling me, and I do not know what to pray for to take this torment from me." From that day forward, my life changed.

It took me a long time to realize I had spent most of my life proving others wrong versus enjoying my growth and finding happiness in my journey. The bitterness and anger had taken root in my heart and bloomed destruction. Although the rage fueled my success for years, I'm not proud of it all. I had violated my values, and the people I cared for had been wounded in the process. My undealt past and fears were on a path to destroying everything I worked so hard to achieve. The negative words spoken to me were about to bloom into reality. Imagine self-limiting beliefs so powerful it mutes your confidence and breathes life into your self-destruction. My confidence is now unmuted, and keeping it that way is something I strive for each day. My story is more common than we think, and we often do not talk about it for fear of being viewed as weak. Studies suggest our confidence has a significant impact on performance in the workplace. Self-limiting beliefs cloud our wisdom to see right from wrong and destroy our confidence. When our confidence is attacked, we become less empathetic, have less clarity, and become irritated with the daily demands.[135] In organizational settings, negative thoughts can damage career advancement for fear of one's ability to perform.[136]

Today, you may be facing an inaccurate assumption about your abilities, your worth, and maybe even your existence. You are not alone. Eighty-three percent of the executive women surveyed as part of the H.E.R.A.C.T. research said they experience self-limiting beliefs that impact their confidence. The same women also said trauma played a significant role. Trauma resides in our nervous system and overpoweringly stores itself in every brain area, impacting our thoughts, emotions, and actions. Trauma is an expert at breeding seeds of self-limiting beliefs. These thoughts take root inside us, hold on to the past, and manipulate our confidence to build our future. But you did not get this far to give up; it is time to build your confidence.

The McKinsey & Company centered leadership research reports more women in the workplace are a factor in the U.S. economy's success. Still, the same study shows self-limiting beliefs stand in the way of a women's success.[137] Self-limiting

---

[135] Dickerson, A., & Taylor, M. A. (2000). Self-limiting behavior in women: Self-esteem and self-efficacy as predictors. *Group & Organization Management, 25*(2), 191-210. doi:10.1177/1059601100252006.

[136] Ibid

[137] Barsh, J. & Yee, L. (2011). Unlocking the full potential of women in the US economy. *McKinsey & Company,* (April).

boliofc do not discriminate. They will attack equally the strong and the weak. We are all a target, and guarding our confidence and staying vigilant is something we must do daily. It is essential to note significant organizational and cultural norms fail to recognize women's potential. But, that is a topic for another book, not a chapter. The truth is when a woman can overcome self-limiting beliefs, her confidence rises, and she walks into limitless possibilities.

PRACTICAL EXERCISE

Leverage your failures to thrive in your future.

- Make a List identify three past failures.

1. _____

2. _____

3. _____

- How have these failures impacted your confidence?
- Now, take the time to understand and write down what you learn from them.
- How do these failures benefit you in the future?

HOW YOU SHOW UP MATTERS

How you show up matters, whether you like it or not. Self-confidence is not your ability to look tough or be arrogant. Self-confidence is a fundamental leadership ingredient and critical competence.[138] Self-confidence will fuel you with strength when you need it most. How you perceive yourself influences your

---

[138] Northouse, P.J. (2016). *Leadership Theory and Practice*, *7th edition*, Oaks, CA: Sage Publications, Inc., 23.

confidence.[139] However, confidence does not equal competence or accuracy. Some of the components of confidence include self-efficacy, hope, optimism, and resilience."[140] Self-confidence shows up in your courage to take action—knowing whether you win or lose, you will grow.

Self-confidence will guide our steps towards our dreams and determine how we impact the marketplace.[141] Unfortunately, when compared to men, confidence continues to be a struggle for most women.[142] You have probably heard women will not apply for a job if they do not meet 100 percent of the credentials, while men will apply for the role even if they only meet 50 percent of the requirements. Sadly, for women in the workplace, performance and self-confidence are not enough; they must also demonstrate prosocial behavior.[143] According to Nancy Eisenberg, prosocial behavior refers to voluntary that benefits others. It is crucial to note gender equality and leadership constitute a significant concern in corporate America. However, I will not elaborate on this topic in this book. Instead, I will continue to concentrate on things you can immediately control, your self-confidence, how to achieve it, and sustain it.

[139] Bonner, B.L. & Bolinger, A.R. (2013). Separating the confident from the correct: Leveraging member knowledge in groups to improve decision making and performance. *Organizational Behavior and Human Decision Processes*, 122(2), 214-221.

[140] Archer, S. & Yates, J. (2017). Understanding potential career changers' experience of career confidence following a positive psychology based coaching programme. *Coaching: An International Journal of Theory, Research and Practice*, 10(2), 157-175.

[141] Guillén, L., Mayo, M., & Karelaia, N. (2018). Appearing self-confident and getting credit for it: Why it may be easier for men than women to gain influence at work. *Human Resource Management*, 57(4), 839-854. https://onlinelibrary.wiley.com/doi/10.1002/hrm.21857

[142] Kay, K., & Shipman, C. (2014). The confidence gap. The Atlantic, 14(1), 1-18. Retrieved from: https://www.theatlantic.com/magazine/archive/2014/05/the-confidence-gap/359815/

[143] Guillén, L., Mayo, M., & Karelaia, N. (2018). Appearing self confident and getting credit for it: Why it may be easier for men than women to gain influence at work. *Human Resource Management*, 57(4), 839-854. https://onlinelibrary.wiley.com/doi/10.1002/hrm.21857

OUR EMOTIONS INFLUENCE OUR ACTIONS

Emotional intelligence, otherwise known as emotional quotient or EQ, is essential for exercising confidence. EQ is unlike the intelligence quotient (IQ). Our intellectual and academic qualifications can be measured through our IQ. However, emotional intelligence estimates different kinds of intellect. EQ goes beyond academics and measures our ability to manage emotions.[144] Studies reveal we operate from an emotional and rational mind. Our emotions influence our reactions to cry, laugh, anger, or run. The harmony within them enables us to have a more fulfilling life.[145]

Studies confirm that although you may be the brightest leader in the room, a highly EQ leader will be the most valued and productive leader.[146] Our emotions hold great power and cannot be ignored; IQ means nothing if emotions are not controlled.[147] An unhealthy balance of emotions can cause low self-awareness and burnout, ultimately impacting our relationships.[148]

PRACTICAL EXERCISE

Our EQ increases the more we become aware of our feelings. The journey to developing our EQ is different for everyone.

- You can begin to work on your EQ by learning from others with a high EQ.

---

[144] Singh, D. (2006) *Emotional Intelligence at Work, A Professional Guide.* Thousand Oaks, CA: Response Books.
[145] Ibid
[146] Ibid
[147] Goleman, D. (1994) Emotional Intelligence, Why It Can Matter More Than IQ. New York, NY: Bantam Dell.
[148] Scazzero, P. (2015). *The emotionally healthy leader: How transforming your inner life will deeply transform your church, team, and the world.* Grand Rapids, MI: Zondervan.

- Take notes of people with high EQ, model their behavior, and tweak it as you experience it until you find what works for you.
- Take notice of the triggers causing your emotions to spiral.
- Recognize them and be proactive and intentional about managing your response.
- Take the time to ask for feedback on how you handled a specific situation from someone with a high EQ.
- Focus on the input and intentionally improve your EQ until you master it and it becomes natural.[149]

EQ also is measurable in an organization's culture. Gone are the days when people are asked to leave their personal problems at home. There is only one of you, and anything that affects you will impact your output at home and in the marketplace. Your issues also are the organization's matters. Organizations that lead in this area understand emotional trust and genuine care for the team ensures their employees' well-being.

The greater your EQ, the more control you have over your emotions. The more power you have over your feelings, the more confident you are about your decision-making.

SELF-EFFICACY

Self-efficacy is linked to less fear and reduced anxiety.[150] "High self-efficacy facilitates performance, and successful performance nurtures self-efficacy,"[151] said psychologist Albert Bandura.

[149] Singh, D. (2006) *Emotional Intelligence at Work, A Professional Guide*. Thousand Oaks, CA: Response Books.
[150] Markway, G. (2018, September 20). Why self-confidence is more important than you think. Retrieved February 23, 2021, from https://www.psychologytoday.com/us/blog/shyness-is-nice/201809/why-self-confidence-is-more-important-you-think
[151] Bandura, A. (1997). Self-Efficacy: The exercise of control. New York: Freeman.

Bandura defines self-efficacy as the ability to have self-confidence in ourselves to succeed. In Bandura's social cognitive theory, self-efficacy plays a significant role in our perception of ourselves, our actions, and the achievements of life's goals.[152] Our sense of self-efficacy begins in early childhood and continues throughout our life. Our environment and experiences contribute to the ability to believe in ourselves. People with high self-confidence are typically more engaged, take more risks, and see failure as an opportunity for growth.

In contrast, people with self-limiting beliefs do not have confidence in their capabilities. These individuals place a high focus on failures and avoid stepping out of their comfort zone. Others believe in the motto, "Fake it until you make it," as a survival skill. However, I think standing in our truth is more empowering. Yes, it takes courage and vulnerability to say, "I do not know how, but I can learn, and I will find a way." I have faked it, and I have been honest. Being honest has been more liberating because I could ask questions and never feel I had to cover the lie that I did not know. I know firsthand when I have said I don't know; it makes it easier for others to shut the door. The reality is they did not want me there in the first place, and my truth empowers me. When you walk in your truth, it shows. Your confidence will be an integral part of achieving your dreams, yet it isn't easy to find without a solid foundation to build self-confidence. Building your self-confidence is a journey, and when you step into self-confidence, you grasp the strength of your power.

[152] Dickerson, A. & Taylor, M. A. (2000). Self-limiting behavior in women: Self-esteem and self-efficacy as predictors. *Group & Organization Management, 25*(2), 191-210. doi:10.1177/1059601100252006.

PRACTICAL EXERCISE

Several tools can be leveraged to measure your General Self-Efficacy Scale (GSE). You can google GSE and find several tools to meet your needs. However, you can start by asking yourself these questions.

- Are you confident in your capability to achieve your goals?
- Are your emotional responses balanced when handling unexpected events?
- Do you bounce back fairly quickly after difficult situations?
- Are you usually able to find solutions?
- Do you keep trying even when things get tough?
- Do you perform well even under pressure?

If you answered yes to most of the questions, you would likely have a strong self-efficacy.[153] If you answered no to most of these questions, it is time to take a more thorough look at your actions.

- To improve self-efficacy, some steps you can take include:
  - Recognize and celebrate your small wins, even if no one else celebrates them with you.
  - Set realistic goals.

You can't wake up one day and fly a plane if you never took lessons. It starts with small steps. Remember, your vision should be bold, but the goals you set must be measurable and realistic to achieve your vision.

---

[153] Romppel M, Herrmann-lingen C, Wachter R., et al. (2013) A short form of the General Self-Efficacy Scale (GSE-6). Psychosoc Med. 2013;10:Doc01. doi:10.3205/psm000091.

- Be intentional about managing your emotions.
- Be intentional about managing your thoughts. Speak words of life.
- Take an in-depth look at your life quarterly and look for themes that may be causing the insecurities you believe to be true in your life at that moment. Getting to the root cause sooner than later will enable you to sustain your confidence.

SPIRITUAL CONNECTION

Mark, the evangelist in the New Testament, tells us about an anonymous woman bleeding for 12 years. The story tells she had visited many doctors and experienced horrible things. However, the doctors could not find a cure. After many medical treatment failures, she took the matter into her hands. Despite the lack of answers, she did not give up.

Imagine her condition after 12 years of uncontrollable hemorrhaging. When someone loses blood, they experience weakness, shortness of breath, headaches, dizziness, and irregular heartbeats. The culture considered her legally unclean during those times and exiled her. The story tells she thought to herself, "If only I may touch His clothes, I shall be made well." Anyone in her condition would not have the strength to walk, yet her will and determination were more prevailing than her flesh. She recognized her worth. She knew she was worth fighting for and was willing to walk through the shadow of death and take the chance to reach Jesus. She did not stop searching for healing. It was not up to society to decide her future, and living in agony was not an option for her. She moved through the crowd and touched Jesus' garment in her weakness. When she felt his garment, scripture tells the fountain of blood immediately dried up and healed her of the affliction. In Jesus, she found healing. Jesus said to her, "Daughter, your faith has made you well. Go in peace and be healed of your affliction."

The woman refused to become a victim of her circumstance. Her self-advocacy brought her to the hands of the healer. Imagine the peace and gratitude she felt as she received physical and emotional healing. If she had become a victim of her circumstances, she would have never found peace.

THE COMPANY YOU KEEP INFLUENCES YOUR CONFIDENCE

Humans are naturally relational beings. The interactions, connections, and relationships with others impact our self-confidence. When relational independence becomes part of how we think about ourselves, changes to our self-confidence occur. Studies confirm people with higher positive relational interdependence have more confidence.[154]

IN REAL LIFE: WE CAN PROTECT OUR CONFIDENCE

Even a stranger can shift your confidence. I had received positive feedback from my leadership and was confident I was doing a fantastic job managing work and home. My assistant worked her magic and blocked off my afternoon. Filled with joy, I closed out the day and left work early to pick up the kids at school. Amid my excitement that I was finally able to pick up

---

[154] Gabriel, S., Renaud, J.M., & Tippin, B. (2007). When I think of you, I feel more confident about me: The relational self and self-confidence. *Journal of Experimental Social Psychology, 43*(5), 772-779. https://doi.org/10.1016/j.jesp.2006.07.004

my children from school on this day, another mother says to me, "I have never seen you at the children's activity. Are you one of the kids' moms?" The statement alone was enough to deflate my confidence and send my emotions spiraling. Hundreds of thoughts went through my mind within seconds. Should I explain I'm a working mother? Should I say a wise remark or ignore her existence?

However, I recognized the emotional trigger and knew this was an excellent opportunity to practice my EQ. I replied, "Hello, lovely to meet you as well; my name is Dr. Merary Simeon, the proud mother of Neryah and Marcel, as my children ran into my arms, screaming at the tops of their lungs, "Mommy, I love you, Mommy." Wow! Having them scream "I love you" for the whole world jump-started my confidence. Changes to your self-confidence can waver if you do not know who you are. I'm blessed to be the mother of our children, I know I do great work, and I have to be intentional about protecting my confidence, peace, and joy.

IN REAL LIFE: CONFIDENCE IN YOURSELF MATTERS

As a child, Paula was loved and spoiled by her parents. Paula's confidence radiated through her eyes and in every word. Sadly, in her teenage years, her parents divorced, and her self-confidence shattered. Paula joined a volleyball team, and her skills boosted her confidence. Shortly after joining the team, she sprained her ankle and became depressed. Her self-confidence was once again lost. Paula began to make mistakes that she was not proud of and decided to follow in her brother's footsteps and join the military. Paula's platoon gave her confidence in the military, and she began to feel like her old self. When Paula came home from serving her country, she spent time with her grandmother volunteering in the community. Paula felt inspired, and her confidence rose when giving back to the community. When Paula spent time with her friends from college, Paula felt less important. Paula's situations and relationships determined her self-confidence. Paula did not have confidence in herself and needed the assurance of others. Many of us allow our situations and relationships to affect our self-confidence. Unfortunately, this is a recipe for disaster.

Self-confidence building begins at an early age; most toddlers have extreme confidence in their parents, and their security makes them feel untouchable. When children find themselves in a different environment, their belief in themselves decreases, and self-doubt takes over. Throughout life, people, situations, and settings will influence your confidence.

When we lack self-confidence, we experience anxiety, the feeling of inadequacy, and engage in unhealthy habits. A person raised in a troubled home may lack the confidence to be a good spouse and avoid marriage. A woman may lack confidence and decide not to apply for the next significant role. An expectant mother may feel anxiety because she lacks the confidence to care for her child and terminates her pregnancy. A woman told she was not smart enough may lack the confidence to enroll in school. An executive may experience stress and overwork herself because she lacks confidence in succeeding. A person may lose their employment and lose their self-confidence in finding a better opportunity. Countless scenarios impact one's self-confidence. Our confidence is power, and the reality is there is no confidence without uncertainty. When we are confident, the unknown becomes the familiar ground.

Doubt and self-confidence can co-exist as long as the unknown fills you with the curiosity to learn and to grow. Doubt can stall your growth if you are not paying attention, but faith will enable you to arise and to shine from fear. Trusting and knowing that breakdowns will lead to breakthroughs will make you more confident each day.

PRACTICAL EXERCISE

Answer the following questions about yourself.

- Do you feel confident when you achieve your goals?
- Do you lose your confidence when you are around other people?
- Have you ever walked into a meeting where you were the only one who looked different and felt your confidence drop?
- Who are the people in your circle that cause your confidence to waivers when they are around?
  - Why do you think that is?
- Can you remember a time when your confidence was high?
  - Who was in the room?
  - Who were you talking to at the time?
  - Was someone saying something about you or your work?
  - Why was your confidence high?
- Do you know what moves you to push forward?
- Be honest. Do you know who and what controls your self-confidence, if not you?
- What can you start doing today to build your confidence?

Sadly, there are too many examples to count of famous and wealthy people who appear confident in public due to their worldly status. Some put a high value on their relationship with money, talent, or assets. Yet, many lack the confidence to believe they are enough and end up in self-destruction. For many, bank accounts or education define their self-confidence, only to discover the power of self-confidence does not live in the world but within you.

IN REAL LIFE: WE GROW FROM OUR MISTAKES AND RETORE OUR CONFIDENCE

Marissa was only 10 years old when she decided to break the family cycle. Marissa swore her family would not live paycheck to paycheck. Her confidence could not be shaken despite the numerous obstacles she faced throughout her life. Having achieved her goal at 30 years old, Marissa felt accomplished and became comfortable. Marissa's audacious goal she continued to knock out of the park, gave her confidence, but her comfort zone opened the doors to fear, doubt, and insecurity.

It was clear anything she put her mind to, she would accomplish. In this case, goals drove her confidence. Nothing wrong with that, right? Not quite. Self-confidence in achieving your goals is critical, but knowing and growing from failure will fuel your confidence each time. Marissa failed miserably at being a friend, a daughter, and a partner. Marissa's focus on achieving financial goals made her blind to life and, in turn, made her miss out on the one thing confidence cannot compete against—time. Time with loved ones, time for her well-being, time for love.

Self-confidence is not about crushing goals. Self-confidence is also knowing it is OK to enjoy the journey. In the end, sharing your journey with a friend and loved ones is much sweeter. Marissa's confidence suffered when she began to realize she had destroyed many meaningful relationships while achieving her dream. Marissa's lack of self-confidence to build relationships pushed her away from her loved ones. Marissa's loneliness caused her to lose focus, and it put at risk all the wealth she achieved. Marissa lost trust in her abilities, and it impacted her self-confidence. Marissa's growth opportunity was to learn from her mistakes and invest in her relationships while continuing her success. It is possible to have a career, be financially stable, be a healthy woman, and spend quality time with loved ones.

IN REAL LIFE: SELF-CONFIDENCE EMPOWERS YOU

Uncertainty filled her future. Corporate America was all she knew. Straight out of college, she landed her dream job in a Fortune 100 company. She worked hard and moved up the ladder early in her career. Her goal was to become a CEO. She could never imagine leaving corporate America. One day as she planned her family holiday vacation, she received a call from the office for an important early meeting. Sarah had been through many company-wide restructures, but it never dawned on her she would be impacted negatively. She typically achieves a promotion during a restructuring. Sarah was confident nothing adverse would happen. Sarah was only 42 years of age, her performance was stellar, and her career was thriving. As she opened the door, she thought to herself, it is never good news when your leader and human resources are waiting for you in a conference room.

To flatten the organizational structure, the company decided to eliminate Sarah's position. The uncertainty frightened Sarah. If performance no longer differentiated her from the rest, how can she ensure the next company would not do the same to her? Sarah was confident in her capabilities and had a difficult decision to make. She must choose to contact executive recruiters and go back to what she knew or do something completely different and become an entrepreneur. Either decision was uncertain; corporate America would provide Sarah a weekly stable paycheck. Instead, she talked to her family and consulted with God, mentors, coaches, and friends. Sarah's self-confidence and her loved one's support opened the door for her to pursue entrepreneurship and fulfill her dream of becoming CEO. Sarah would tell me it was not easy, but she also said, "It was all worth it." Today, she is a thriving entrepreneur and loving every minute of it. Sarah did not let the organization's decision impact her future. She turned the uncertainty into a business plan. She over-delivered as she would have if corporate America employed her. Today, her legacy goes beyond corporate America.

Lack of self-confidence shows up in different ways. Sometimes lack of self-confidence may feel like fear, rejection, shame, sadness, loneliness, and hopelessness. Self-confidence feels like acceptance, courage, joy, and strength to move forward despite the unknown. The good news is you can achieve self-confidence despite your failures and experiences. You do not have to live out the rest of your life experiencing depression, hopelessness, and shame. It is time to awaken your self-confidence. Achieving self-confidence and maintaining it will enable you to unleash the best version of yourself.

SPIRITUAL CONNECTION

In the book of Psalms, David says, "Some trust in chariots and some in horses, but we will remember and trust in the name of the Lord our God. They have bowed down and fallen, but we have risen and stood upright." Many will proudly say they trust in the Lord. Their confidence would suggest otherwise—when individuals do not have a deep relationship with Christ, their confidence wavers. They cannot stand in their power because they see themselves through a lens of defeat versus a coherent lens. Feeling left out of a particular group in society also impacts your confidence. Your confidence suffers because you see yourself through society's lens instead of how God sees you, a conqueror.

IN REAL LIFE: FINDING THE CONFIDENCE TO REBUILD IS POSSIBLE

Ariel is a registered nurse with over 20 years of experience. Ariel grew up in a Christian home and always found strength in her relationship with Jesus. Giving birth to her first child was an answered prayer and a joyful day. But her husband quickly stole from her the joy of having a child by attacking her self-confidence. Her husband took no time to attack the way her body looked after giving birth to their beautiful, healthy child. He constantly reminded Ariel her body had changed for the worse. Ariel struggled to lose weight, and it destroyed her confidence. She only saw a weight gain and stretch marks. She could not see the privilege of a mother because she had allowed him to crush her self-confidence. Her diminishing self-confidence pushed Ariel to hold hands with sin each day. As time passed by, she spent less time with God. Her husband made her feel ugly and insecure not only through words but through his infidelity. Ariel had enough, the disloyalty was too much to bear, and she found the strength to separate from her husband. Yet, it was not enough. She continued to struggle with her confidence. A spirit of envy began to rule her mind; she wanted to be like other people because she did not feel worthy.

Years later, she met her second husband, and his words boosted her confidence until the honeymoon was over. Her second husband became mentally and physically abusive. Each day the abuse she endured dimmed her light more and more. Ariel turned to pill addiction to quiet the mental and physical pain, a destructive habit that put her profession at risk. She focused her energy on masking her addiction. People saw her as a happy person and did not notice her deep pain.

Ariel could no longer mask the pain and loneliness. She screamed and cried out to God but could not hear His voice. Ariel yearned to listen to His voice and began to seek Him in prayer and scripture. In the darkest moments, in her closet, she rebuilt her relationship with Christ. Ariel said, "I was tired of being sick and tired." She turned to God and asked him to strip her away from her sin and give her the strength to move forward. On September 21, 2019, God gave Ariel the power to stop drug addiction. The more time Ariel spent in her prayer closet, the more confident she became. She was unstoppable; the authority and power she felt empowered her to march forward with confidence and own her narrative.

When Ariel walked away from the pill addiction, the vale blocking her clarity lifted. Ariel's spiritual eyes and ears were now open, and she could clearly hear God's voice. Ariel grew stronger spiritually, physically, and mentally. She began to work out in her room and write affirmations in the mirror. Ariel's husband would claim she was going crazy, but in fact, her future had never been clearer. While close friends would encourage her not to leave her husband because she would struggle financially, her faith was in God. Ariel divorced her second husband and found peace, joy, and purpose in Christ. Time has passed, and Ariel continues to thrive; she has not struggled financially, and the pill addiction is behind her. Ariel said, "God was there ready to ignite my power, I only needed to trust in him, and my confidence grew."

During the COVID-19 pandemic, patients were not allowed to be visited by family. Ariel found purpose in helping the patients heal from the inside out, praying with them, and sharing the good news of Christ. Ariel is incredibly aware self-confidence is a journey. To maintain her self-confidence, she prays, worships, continues to write affirmations, and surrounds herself with like-minded people who inspire her to be her best self. While the road is not always easy, she is ready to conquer one day at a time.

To be self-confident means to love yourself despite your imperfections. Self-confidence is not prideful, is not loud, and is not attention-seeking. Self-confidence is knowing your worth and acting as such. As women, we must be brave enough to know we are more than our bodies. We can point fingers at our past and the systems designed to keep us down. Still, nothing is going to change unless we do. As we find our confidence, it is critical to help other women rise. Everyone is fighting a battle, but not everyone is equipped to fight it. As you strengthen in your transformation, please pay it forward. Do not criticize her; pray for her, help her make the right connections, and help her rise and shine, expecting nothing in return. Women can be each other's own worst critics. Ultimately, it says way more about how they feel about themselves than others. Confident women don't tear each other down—they support each other. Confident women will demand justice for you when you are not in the room. Confident women know their sisters' worth.

The key to self-confidence begins with the word "self." Confidence is not found through external validation but comes from within—a genuine acceptance of both your flaws and strengths, knowing you are forgiven in God's eyes. Perfectionism is the opposite of confidence—it will cause you to question yourself, to overthink, and to stall. The cost of procrastination and fear of failure is much greater than trying, failing, and growing.

REBUILDING YOUR CONFIDENCE

Confidence grows as a result of your actions. Despite all that goes on around us, there are many things that we cannot control, but you can manage your actions. To build or rebuild self-confidence, you must know where you stand, acknowledge how you genuinely feel, and know where you want to go. Self-awareness will allow you to flag the situations, people, and feelings that impact your self-confidence. Achieving comfort and avoiding the problem is not the goal. The goal is to be aware and to continue to push forward, knowing fear, self-doubt, nervousness, and many more feelings are part of the process. Many times we run from our feelings because it hurts to face them. However, to build your confidence, you must acknowledge the pain. Understanding how you got to where you are today and what self-confidence looks like will give you the knowledge needed to rebuild your confidence.

PRACTICAL EXERCISE

As you begin to identify the thoughts, situations, and feelings that diminish your self-confidence, consider these steps.

- Can you link the shift in your self-confidence to a situation, person, or place?
  - What is the situation?
- Identify and list how the thoughts and feelings make you feel about yourself.
- Recognize that while the feelings are real, they are not always correct.
  - Challenge what the thoughts and feelings say about you.
- Replace each thought with positive affirmations.
- Take a balanced approach and ask yourself:
  - What is the worse scenario that could happen?
  - What is the best thing that could happen?
  - What is the one thing I can do right now to begin to build my confidence?

SPIRITUAL CONNECTION

In 2 Samuel 9, we learn of Mephibosheth. Mephibosheth was the grandson of King Saul, the first king of Israel. He was a prince. However, he was only a child when King Saul died. The nanny heard the news of the king's death and Mephibosheth's father and panicked. She ran out of the palace with Mephibosheth. In the panic, the child fell to the ground and became crippled for the rest of his life. Mephibosheth lost his grandfather, father, family, wealth, and the ability to walk without assistance again. One day, King David asked if anyone from King Saul's lineage was alive? Mephibosheth was still alive and was now living in a place called Lo Debar.

Lo Debar means a dry place—a place with no dreams and no fruit. During his time in Lo Debar, he stayed at the house of Ammiel. Ammiel signifies "God is my father." Although Mephibosheth was going through a dark time, God had not forgotten him. When King David found him, he asked if he would like to come and live in the palace, and Mephibosheth said yes. King David then gave him all the land that once belonged to his grandfather, Saul. He also gave him servants to work the land and bring Mephibosheth all the fruits of the labor with the only request for Mephibosheth to eat at the king's table each day.

If you have lost your confidence in a better tomorrow, Mephibosheth represents you. Ammiel today signifies, "God the Father is with you." God is waiting for you to come and to eat at His table. When you seek God's kingdom and His righteousness, all the things and so much more than you can ever imagine also will be given to you. We all have the right to live out God's promises for us. God's promises are for everyone, but it requires action on our part. It requires you to invite Him and to accept Him in your life. It does not matter how much self-confidence you possess. One thing is sure with Christ; you will exceed your dreams. He is the King of Glory, and His promises belong to those who love Him. King David restored all that Mephibosheth lost and more. Remember, you are the daughter of the King of Kings; He can restore your confidence and so much more.

H.E.R.A.C.T.

CHAPTER 7:

TRANSFORMATION

"We possess within ourselves at every moment
of our lives, under all circumstances, the power to
transform the quality of our lives."

~ Werner Erhard

Self-transformation is not a one-time event; transformation requires changes in you. To sustain your transformation, you must have a relationship with Christ. Anyone can change short-term, but living a life in Christ will sustain your transformation. Our lives will transform positively or negatively whether we decide to take the driver's seat or not. We choose the long-term results of our actions. More than ever, we need to exercise our talents. It is critical to invest in the H.E.R.A.C.T. transformation journey. Healing is necessary to achieve transformation; if you skip the healing process, it will block every step of your transformation journey. For your perspective to change, you have to face your past.

STRIVE TO REACH THE "UNCOMFORTABLE ZONE"

Change is difficult and uncomfortable. Be patient; it takes time. Each day push yourself out of your comfort zone. Set an appointment each day with your Creator, Jesus Christ, to get to know Him personally. What is the worst thing that can happen if you build a relationship with Him? What is the best thing that can happen? If transformations were comfortable, everyone would be living their best life, achieving their dreams, weighing at their ideal weight, thriving in relationships, and experiencing peace with their past.

Too many of us use our gifts to create division and to influence others and become their worse selves. Leadership comes with significant accountability "for whom much is given; much will be required." How we lead our life carries a long-lasting impact on lives we will never know. Your ability to maintain flexibility and transform, while staying true to your values, will be critical in your transformation journey.

Navigating uncertainty can be scary, but do not fear because God is always with you. Through your transformation journey, discernment is essential to ensure you are walking the right path. Scripture reminds us in Romans 12, "Do not be conformed to this world, but be transformed by the renewal of your mind, that by testing you may discern what the will of God is, what is right and acceptable and perfect." Knowledge is not transformation; your actions will dictate your daily transformation level. Discerning the voice of God through your journey will ensure peace. It does not say it will be easy, but knowing God's voice and taking action will bring you victory and give God glory. How do you know if you are taking the proper steps? If you are out of peace, you are not in the presence of God. If you depart from the presence of God, your transformation will be temporary.

Self-transformation requires discipline. Busyness is artificial significance. Being intentional about your transformation is life-changing. Through self-discipline, you have the power to recognize right from wrong and choose the right path. Abraham Lincoln once said, "Discipline is choosing between what you want now and what you want most." To empower your discipline, you must first understand your weaknesses, what slows you down or blocks your transformation. Denying the need for change will extend the journey. Standing in denial will only hinder your transformation. While the transformation does not occur overnight, your commitment to the process will supersede your flesh's calling for you to quit.

If you seek long-term transformation, you make God your partner in your journey. Choose your actions wisely.

IN REAL LIFE: WE ASK FOR HELP

Self-transformation requires you to be humble and recognize when you need help. There is a significant difference between a strong woman and a woman of power. Connie's mother raised her to be an independent woman. Connie was resilient. There was nothing she could not manage in high school, college, and career. One day, depression attacked. It was a feeling she had never experienced. After many failed attempts to take on depression independently, she realized she did not have the strength to fight the battle alone and knew she needed reinforcement.

THE OTHER SIDE OF TRANSFORMATION

Between the fear and emotions, Connie found the strength to

seek help. At that moment, Connie began to transform from a strong woman to a woman of power. A woman of power realizes she cannot do it on her own. She understands being strong and intelligent means nothing if your mind and soul have no peace. To walk in power is to set your pride aside; it is to leave the bitterness behind and take the time to heal to rise stronger. A strong woman will endure a toxic relationship. A woman of power will walk away with nothing; knowing her worth will enable her to rebuild a significantly better life. A strong woman moves through life alone, breaking barriers. A woman of power brings others along and does not get tired of doing good.

Transformations are painful and take time, but a change is required to rise to the next level and to thrive in your marriage, purpose, and marketplace. Changes will continue to challenge us rapidly, and our power is our ability to transform.[155] Every person can transform; only one critical ingredient is needed: your willingness to change. A breakthrough occurs when you understand and face the self-limiting beliefs—when the limiting beliefs no longer control you, transformation occurs. Psychologist Jeffrey A Kottler says, "Once you become more aware of your patterns, you can significantly enhance the magnitude, power, and peace of the changes you'd like to make."[156] Your next steps will determine if you continue to carry around limiting beliefs and settle for less or go after the life God promised you. God has already promised to restore what is rightfully yours and more. Wait no more. Your best life starts today. Tomorrow is not promised; activate your power and start your transformation journey.

[155] Kegan, R. & Lahey, L.L. (2009). *Immunity to change: how to overcome it and unlock potential in yourself and your organization. Boston,* MA: Harvard Business Press.
[156] Kottler, J.A. (2013). Change: *What really leads to lasting personal transformation.* Oxford University Press, Incorporated.

WE CAN ALL BENEFIT FROM A CHANGE PLAN

Dr. John Kotter is an expert in leading change and the author of *Leading Change*. He is best known for the eight steps to transforming an organization.[157]

1. Step One: Create Urgency.
2. Step Two: Form a Powerful Coalition.
3. Step Three: Create a Vision for Change.
4. Step Four: Communicate the Vision.
5. Step Five: Remove Obstacles.
6. Step Six: Create Short-Term Wins.
7. Step Seven: Build on the Change.
8. Step Eight: Anchor the Changes.

While these steps are common in corporate America, one can argue the eight steps apply to self-transformation. However, I would make one exception. I would add self-commitment to transformation as the pre-requisite to Step One. The change will only be temporary unless you intentionally invest in every part of your brokenness. Step One refers to the idea of creating urgency or demand. For change to occur, there must be a demand. To understand the demand, you must analyze the need. You must ask yourself where I would be if I continue with this behavior, this situation, or in this environment. To be open to change, you must be willing to be vulnerable and truthful with yourself. You must be ready to want to change those painful areas you have been ignoring for so long. The demand for change may be triggered by trauma or an area you want to grow. The key is you

---

[157] Kotter, J.P. (2012). *Leading Change with a New Preface by the Author*, Boston, MA: Harvard Business Review Press.

have to want change, you may not like the process, but it works.

The second step requires you to build a powerful alliance to support you through the change. From healing to fulfilling your vision, you must identify accountability partners, mentors, and friends who will help you move forward. This means surrounding yourself with people and resources who support your self-transformation to a better you. It means inviting God to be part of your transformation journey.

Now that you understand the urgency and have a support group, it is time to create the vision for change. This step is essential because each stage will vary in time, and you will be more likely to fail in the transformation process without a change plan. Your ability to refer back to your transformation plan will quiet down the noise and get you back on track. You are accountable for your actions; you must resist giving up. However, you also have to remain flexible with your plan. The timelines may change, the support system may vary. Still, your goal towards self-transformation and living a life filled with peace, self-love, and purpose should remain.

Communicating the vision is just as important. Sharing your vision with your loved ones and support group helps them understand the reason for your new behavior. It also will enable you to move forward. Any type of transformation is complex, do not go in it alone. Leverage the people around you. If you are alone, join a Bible group or a social media group of women who seek similar interests. Network with like-minded individuals, who will cheer for you throughout your journey.

THE PERILS OF BLIND SPOTS

Removing obstacles is the next step. This step may look like removing yourself from toxic relationships, excuses, or eliminating temptations. In this phase, asking for help is a must because removing obstacles may not be easy if the hindrance holding you back is a blind spot. Blind spots refer to areas in your life negatively impacting your growth, yet you cannot see.[158] If it makes you feel any better, we all have blind spots. Organizations leverage a wide range of tools to expose possible blind spots as part of leadership development.[159] Do not feel alone; even the most successful leaders have to develop these areas each day. To grasp your blind spots, you will need to frequently and intentionally seek feedback to shine a light on your blind spots. Surround yourself with trusted people; they can help you navigate those areas you cannot see.

Have you experienced driving calmly when, all of a sudden, a car appears next to you out of nowhere? Imagine you are a safe driver and follow all the rules. First, you turn your signal on with ample time to signal you are moving into the next late. Next, you look at your side-view mirrors, and you see no car in your way. When you are about to move into the next lane, the sensor goes on and warns you there is a car next to you. This sensor has successfully helped millions of people avoid fatal accidents. It is the same with our blind spots. We cannot see them, but others close to us can help you identify things you cannot see for yourself.

Scripture warns us about blind spots. God knows our blind spots; He can bring those blind spots to light if we ask Him. Psalm 19:12 states, "Who can understand his errors? Cleanse

---

[158] Bazerman, A. & Tenbrunsel, A. (2011). *Blind Spots, Why We Fail to Do What's Right and What to Do about It.* Princeton, NJ: Princeton University Press.
[159] Van Velsor, E.V., McCauley, C. D., & Ruderman, M. N. (Eds.), 2010. *The Center for Creative Leadership Handbook of Leadership Development* (3rd Ed.) San Francisco, CA. Jossey-Bass.

me from secret faults. Keep back me from arrogant sins; Let the enemy know they do not have dominion over me. Then I shall be blameless, And I shall be innocent of great transgression."

PRACTICAL EXERCISE

- Do you remember the last time you were wrong about something? If it is difficult to remember the last time you made a mistake, you may be at risk of losing a grip on reality.
- Another self-check that comes with a warning is to spend a few hours around a young child; they will shine a light on your blind spots for you and everyone around you to know.
  - The warning here is do not dismiss what the child is saying. Pay attention, do not ignore a child's comments. They are only speaking the truth and mean no harm (most of the time). As parents, we always tell our children to speak the truth, yet we often do not want to hear it when they do.

IN REAL LIFE: WE CAN LEARN OUR BLIND SPOTS

At an extended family dinner, Laila said, "If I do not have coffee in the morning, I am cranky all day." Her 7-year-old daughter quickly replied, "No, mommy, when you go to bed without praying, you typically do not have a good day. When you pray, even if you do not have your coffee right away, you are loving and kind even if I do something you dislike." Everyone on the table gasped, and some said, you should not say that, child. Laila realized the coffee did not make her day, but her intimacy with God filled her with love. Sometimes, children have the most realistic insight because they watch our every move, even when we think they are not paying attention. Do not dismiss a child's comment next time they reveal a blind spot to you.

When you abide in the presence of the Lord, He shows you your blind spots, and you can take action to walk in the light. News flash, you do not need to wait for a child to call you out on your blind spots in front of everyone at the table. You can expose yourself to the truth of Jesus Christ.

The last step is to anchor the change. What does success look like to you each day, each week, each year? Create short-term wins. No milestone is too small. Making it through the day is a perfect milestone depending on your situation. Make sure to celebrate it even if there is no one around. Smile, tell yourself how amazing you are, and keep moving forward. Even in most sports, to get to the championship, you must play one game at a time. The champions win and lose some but ultimately still bring the victory home.

Take the time to assess your progress throughout the process and build on the change as needed. Maybe there are some things you need to modify, stop or start doing. You may even need to reassess or engage your support team differently. Perhaps you need to spend more time in prayer. Whatever it may be, do what works for you. Remember, this is your journey and yours only. Take the time to reassess and check in on your plan.

Finally, anchor the change, remain disciplined, and stick to the process. Stay focused on the goal. Resist going back to the familiar to the old you at every step. "The personal transformations that really stick, that continue to blossom over time are those that become an integrated part of who you are," says Jeffrey A Kottler.[160] There is a reason why you began this transformational journey. If you integrate H.E.R.A.C.T. into your life and engage God as one of your partners, He will enable you to conquer every step of the transformation journey. Anchored in God, you are sure to activate your power, unlock your potential, and fulfill your purpose.

IN REAL LIFE: YOU CAN FIND PEACE AND JOY

Diana, determined to impact her future, began to make changes in her life. She hired a fitness coach, joined a Bible study group, and removed herself from toxic relationships. Diana was doing all the right things by respecting herself, elevating her mindset, and building her spiritual life. Diana had enough motivation to stick to her commitments even when tired. However, she still did not have peace. One day, scripture took her to Matthew 18:22, "I do not say to you, up to seven times, but up to seventy times seven." After reading this verse, Diana's heart became heavy, and anger came over her. She did not want to forgive the person who caused her pain many years ago. She let it go and went on with her life. Still, the lack of peace made her days harder spiritually, mentally, emotionally, and physically. The turmoil was too much to bear, and Diana felt convicted and ready to forgive. When Diana forgave from the bottom of her heart, the weight lifted off her. Immediately she felt joy and more determined than ever to step into the next level.

All change takes time. Big or small, change deserves reflection, attention, and intention. You do not need to go through self-transformation alone. I recommend you invite Christ to be your

---

[160] Kottler, J.A. (2013). Change: What really leads to lasting personal transformation. Oxford University Press, Incorporated.

partner and guide in our transformation. God will heal every aspect of your brokenness, but you have to be willing to hand it all over to Him. Scripture has captured over 7,000 promises God has made to you. He has not changed His mind; His word is truth. God continues to be a father of action, a friend, a mentor, a guide, and a protector. Having the Creator of the universe as your partner during your transformation will give you authority, love, innovation, wisdom, peace, and strength for the journey. There is no downside to inviting God into your life. You can only benefit from a relationship with the Creator.

ACTIVATE THE DEVINE – AND DO GREAT THINGS

Your transformation starts with you. Own your transformation and do not delegate your authority. Fear is a tactic the enemy uses to keep your light from shining. Demand fear to take a back seat and keep its mouth shut. As your transformation nourishes, remember your talents will not be enough to sustain it. Do not conform to the patterns of this world. Seek the kingdom of God first. Make seeking God a daily practice in your life. God wants you to thrive. Do not worry about what others think. Worry about wasting your life's purpose. In Christ, you can find joy even in the most challenging circumstances. You are valuable, gifted, and have a kingdom purpose on this earth.

Scriptures tell us in 2 Timothy 2, "Be diligent to present yourself approved to God, a worker who does not need to be ashamed, rightly dividing the word of truth." The beauty of partnering with God is you can ensure your purpose is His will in your life and not your own. Paul believed he was honoring God by persecuting Christians. He leveraged his strength in knowledge to bring to life his purpose. He had a following and led multitudes down the wrong path. However, Paul's encounter with God on the road to Damascus revealed Paul's real purpose. Paul now looked at his education from a different view, and it all made perfect sense. Paul was educated by the best during his time. Yet did not achieve a deep understanding of the word until his encounter with Christ. Paul then leveraged his strength to fearlessly and passionately fulfill God's purpose in him. Are you leveraging your strengths to do God's will or your will? As a Christian leader, you must align with God's purpose or run the risk of leading your loved ones, teams, and business towards devastation. Paul says, "That the wisdom of this world is foolishness." Every action you take exposes your character and reveals who you really are in Christ.

In the book Change: *What really leads to lasting personal transformation*, Jeffrey Kottler, professor, psychologies, and consultant, provides six different levels to change what he believes leads to long-term transformation. In his book, he includes our ability to change our attitudes to one of acceptance and patience as well as our ability to shift our attention and explore new behaviors to achieve a better you. Another level of change Kottler discusses is our ability to develop resiliency, build a support system, reframe our thoughts and find a higher purpose. Kottler's level of change supports the H.E.R.A.C.T. framework. Every aspect of H.E.R.A.C.T. enables your transformation journey to a deeper level. From challenging your self-limiting beliefs to changing your life to achieve your best self, transformation can be both messy and rewarding. Your title does not dictate your wisdom and strength in the transformation. It is the journey in which you will acquire wisdom and self-power. The impact of your transformation is established by whom you serve. Do you submit to the limitations of the flesh or the limitless power of our healer, confidant, creator, and protector?

Much of the world's chaos is due to the lack of self-transformation. Spiritually led leaders, more than ever, are essential to the future of humanity. It is time for Holy Spirit-led leaders to rise in the frontlines, including government, the community, education, healthcare, law, business, and the church. Society is suffering because leaders lead from the limitations of the flesh and lack spiritual ability. Research shows that "spiritual perspectives of human behavior can provide a balanced perspective on all manner of organizational issues."[161]

A spiritual perspective is proven to be effective in the marketplace; imagine what it can do in your personal life. If you allow the Holy Spirit to work in you, the Holy Spirit will transform you from the inside out. Chasing external transformation will make you physically healthy, but only through the Holy Spirit will you experience genuine self-transformation. Your leadership will elevate to a higher level of performance. You will not only transform the marketplace, but you will change the lives of those around you. When God powers you, you have peace. You begin to produce the fruits of the

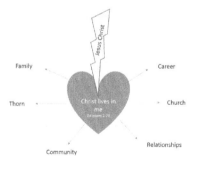

---

[161] Crossman, J. (2010). Conceptualizing spiritual Leadership in secular organizational contexts and its relation to a transformational, servant, and environmental Leadership. *Leadership & Organizational Development.*

Holy Spirit: love, joy, peace, forbearance, kindness, goodness, faithfulness, gentleness, and self-control. Against such things, there is no law.

When the things around you drive you, your life becomes noisy. To awaken your spiritual eyes, ears, and tongue is to step into a higher dimension, a different level of power. Keep in mind a relationship with God does not mean the thorn will go away. It means God will give you peace and strength in your weakness when you abide in Him.

SPIRITUAL CONNECTION

"Therefore, so that I would not become arrogant, a thorn in the flesh was given to me, a messenger of Satan to trouble me—so that I would not become arrogant. I asked the Lord three times about this that it would depart from me. But he said to me, "My grace is enough for you, for my power is made perfect in weakness." So then, I will boast most gladly about my weaknesses so that the power of Christ may reside in me. Therefore, I am content with weaknesses, with insults, with troubles, with persecutions and difficulties for the sake of Christ, for whenever I am weak, then I am strong." [162]

Whatever the thorn represents in your life, know it does not stand in the way of your transformation. While the hurt associated with traumatic events is undeniable, extensive research indicates that many also experience positive changes in the process of overcoming the pain.[163] Many call this today resilience or Post

---

[162] 2 Corinthians 12:7-10, New English Translation Bible
[163] Weiss, T. (2014). Personal transformation: Posttraumatic growth and gerotranscendence. *The Journal of Humanistic Psychology, 54*(2).

Traumatic Growth model, known as PTG. The PTG model investigates constructive changes subsequent traumatic life events. The PTG model indicates the positive changes achieved during stressful times "ultimately leads to increased well-being and life stratification."[164] As a result of a life-changing event, people often ask themselves, "What is my purpose."

When we reflect on who we really are, the blinders are removed in many cases. We can realize that materialistic things will never replace the things of the heart and spirit. The darkness and deep emotional suffering may be what leads to transformation. When you find yourself alone and in the dark, I invite you to ask God to shine a light in your life. Ask Him in your own words right now, do not wait a minute longer. Or you can say this: "God, I invite you into my life; please forgive me for my sins. I accept you as my Lord and Savior. Lord, I need you; shine your light on me." In Christ, we have everything we need to live a life of purpose, and the closer our relationship with God, the greater our growth.

Everything you do requires energy. Science calls "activation energy," the power needed to push a boulder up a hill onto the other side. Anything short of this energy will result in the original state. Can you relate? How many stones are you pushing up the hill today? How many return to the same place? At the beginning of the year, many of us will set a new year resolution to transform our current state. However, within days, most new year resolutions fail. Many of us can identify the demand for personal change. We also can create a clear vision and execution plan. However, most of us lack the sufficient power to see it through.

Most of us become victims of a lifestyle and continue to fail

---

[164] Weiss, T. (2014). Personal transformation: Posttraumatic growth and gerotranscendence. *The Journal of Humanistic Psychology, 54*(2).

despite the many attempts. The most common example is the desire to achieve physical well-being through weight loss. Sadly, most fail to achieve the desired weight loss, fall into depression, or become addicted to drugs and surgery to keep their physical looks. Last but not least is the professional who gives 200 percent but loses valuable time enjoying life and doing what she loves. In all these examples, the person trying to change their condition failed because they lacked the demanded energy needed for change.

What is the amount of activation energy needed to achieve personal transformation? There are two ways to address this question. Either muster the power to create the demanded energy in one try or lower the activation needed, also known as a catalyst.[165] A catalyst can be an individual, object, or event which brings about lasting change. A catalyst, in this case, could be a coach, trainer, mentor, or deity. The catalyst provides the individuals with an energy source outside of their understanding, pushing their limits to the next level. Many try to do it independently, but they lack the discipline to create repeatable positive new habits. God is the catalyst that brings about the desired change. In John 14, we learn God left a helper, the Holy Spirit. "If you love me, keep my commands. And I will ask the Father, and he will give you another advocate to help you and be with you forever— the Spirit of truth. The world cannot accept him because it neither sees nor knows him. But you know him, for he lives with you and will be in you." The Holy Spirit produces a powerful supernatural source of energy.

---

[165] Ravelli, D., Protti, S., & Albini, A. (2015). Energy and molecules from photochemical/photocatalytic reactions. An overview. *Molecules (Basel, Switzerland), 20*(1), 1527-1542.

In the Hebrew language, Ruakh is the living energy source of the Holy Spirit of God. What seems impossible for someone today can be a stepping-stone of victory for tomorrow. Many of us are trying to change a lifetime of conditioning on our own. Still, it leaves us tired and hopeless. Scripture leaves us instructions and calls us to be born again in Christ, meaning putting our flesh (sin/limitation) to rest so that we can see His promise. There are two significant limiting obstacles here on earth: gravity and self-limitation. Gravity is consistent, and we will not discuss it further. However, self-limitation continues to breed more self-doubt and leads us to despair. When one is born again, one can accept the past and surrender to a new foundation laid on the rock, which is Jesus. The Holy Spirit then leads you with the power of heaven to the light of truth here on earth. I can confidently and powerfully proclaim all things through Christ can be achieved. Every time you pull your power from the Holy Spirit, you no longer try to push the stone up the hill. You command the mountain to move with faith, and it will move.

I have been on the battlefield fighting against self-limiting beliefs since 1984, and I did not know it. Inaccurate thoughts of yourself are dangerous and must be strategically defeated. While I have thrived in the face of adversity, self-limiting beliefs held me back for years from achieving my fullest potential. These thoughts imprisoned my mind and kept me from enjoying the fruits of the Spirit. H.E.R.A.C.T. is a life-changing formula for sustainable self-transformation. I'm on a journey to share my learnings and empower every woman to activate her transformation.

The beauty of the application of H.E.R.A.C.T. will empower

every aspect of your life. Our life experiences will not always be pleasant ones. We will encounter people and situations that bring us pain. It is critical to intentionally leverage the H.E.R.A.C.T. to ensure healing and not let unforgiveness live in your heart. The lack of healing creates strongholds that impact our personal, professional and spiritual growth. I make guarding my heart a priority, for out of it flows the issues of our life. Elevating your mindset can translate into something different for everyone, but the concept is the same. We unleash our power when we renew our minds and embrace the challenge. I often imagine the best scenario and analyze the risk of doing nothing. Typically doing nothing does not win the argument. When I saw myself through God's eyes, I learned to respect myself and walk away from toxic environments. Achieving my dreams and walking in my purpose took more than putting one foot forward. It took awaking the confidence in me that had been asleep. When I understood my identity in Christ, I became unstoppable. Sure, it was not easy, but mental, emotional, physical, and spiritual strength accompanied me to win. The transformation from the inside out is the most significant transformation you could achieve. Self-transformation brings you an unexplainable peace that allows you to shine your light in the darkness and bring hope to those living in the dark.

For society's standards, I should have been happy with my accomplishments. However, achievements and time made it apparent success does not equal peace. After many failures, in 2011, I found the secret recipe missing from a sustainable self-transformation—Jesus Christ. Through the Holy Spirit's guidance, I was able to heal, elevate my mind, learn to respect myself, achieve confidence, and transform into the woman I am today. While inaccurate thoughts about myself try to creep up at times, I now can quickly face them, address them and conquer them. You, too, can delight in the fruits of the Spirit and own your narrative.

I believe every woman has powerful, unique gifts planted in her specifically to achieve her divine purpose. Yet, the unwelcome guests are ready and able to destroy us if we permit them. Your commitment to ACTivating H.E.R.A.C.T. in your life will empower you to re-write your story and experience a sustainable, life-changing transformation. My hope is this book plants a seed of healing, hope, and transformation in you. Arise today and choose to ACTivate H.E.R.A.C.T.. You are loved, worthy, and beautifully unique. You are worth the fight. Every step in H.E.R.A.C.T. brings you closer to realizing the best you in every aspect of your life. I want the world to know the secret ingredient is inviting Jesus Christ into your life and abiding in Him. Invest more energy believing in who you are and less on doubting your potential. There is urgency; the world needs the talents you possess; it is time to activate your power, unlock your potential, and fulfill your purpose.

H.E.R.A.C.T.

CHAPTER 8:
LIMITLESS POSSIBILITIES

"He who can do immeasurably more than all we ask or imagine, according to His power that is at work within us."

~ Ephesians 3:20

While I grew up surrounded by a family of faith, I was 38 years old when I gave my life to Jesus Christ. It was then I began the journey to understand the secrets to unleash the power of the Holy Spirit within me. H.E.R.A.C.T. has been transformational in my professional and personal life. It empowered me to activate the power within me. A power that removed the scales blinding me from the truth. I was quenching the power within me, and I had to make a choice. Accepting Jesus Christ into my life was the first step. However, inviting God into your life does not mean the Holy Spirit is free to unleash His power. We often constrain the Holy Spirit and force what we want in our lives instead of what the Holy Spirit desires for us in the marketplace, our ministry, and our family. If you have not experienced the power of the Holy Spirit, you have not activated the power within you. If you are not enjoying the fruits of the spirit, your potential is untapped. The good news is the power within you is like a roaring flame ready, willing, and able to empower your every move.

Succeeding in the workplace is remarkable. Yet, the power of the Holy Spirit has powered me to unlock and walk in my purpose, live in peace with joy, and succeed as a wife, mother, daughter, and executive. Healing set me free, elevating my mindset to see what God has for my life allows me to march forward. Respecting how God sees me gives me the power, wisdom, and strength to achieve my purpose confidently. Only then was I able to hear God's voice and unlock God's purpose in my life, my true purpose on this earth. With the Holy Spirit free to move in me, the storms come into my life, but they do not prosper, and my power, potential, and purpose are limitless.

Today, I am blessed to have a God-fearing husband who submits to God and leads our home with love, wisdom, strength, and courage powered by the Holy Spirit. A few months before we married, God gave me the vision of my husband and me walking on the beach with a happy toddler daughter running on the beach, and in my arms, I held a newborn son. I still feel the peace of looking at my family in the vision. According to society and science, I was at high risk, and after two miscarriages, the chances of having a child were not favorable. I remember calling out to God and reminding him of the vision He gave me. I called on that promise and asked the Holy Spirit to intervene for me. At age 40, I gave birth to our daughter; and age 42, I gave birth to our son. If it were up to me, I would have had more children. However, knowing God knows what is best for us, we were obedient. The vision was clear: a daughter and a son. They are the perfect addition to our family.

I have learned to be obedient to God's will and not my own. The day our son was born, my doctor had called and wanted me to come into her office. When I received the call, I told the nurse; I had an upcoming appointment with the doctor the following week, and I did not need to come in, but the doctor insisted. I felt great and considered not going and, as if the doctor was reading my mind, the doctor's office called again to tell me the doctor wanted to see me immediately. I was a little confused and made the time to go into the doctor's office. When I walked into the doctor's office, she hugged me and told me she could not sleep thinking of me, and she wanted to follow her instincts as a doctor and run some tests. I immediately knew something was wrong, and the Holy Spirit intervened and disturbed her to see me. Moments after the ultrasound, I was rushed to the hospital for an emergency c-section. The amniotic sac was punctured, and I did not realize it and the umbilical cord had several knots. I remember bursting into tears and the vision of our children flashing in my head. A few minutes later, our son was born. I honor and thank God because He keeps His promises when we honor Him. Today, we enjoy our daughter and son.

The peace in our marriage and family does not mean we are perfect or do not have problems. We are far from perfect. It does mean we have peace and a sound mind to face what comes our way. Self-limiting beliefs had me convinced I could not achieve success at work and have a healthy marriage and family. All that changed when I chose to take the steps necessary to remove the obstacles holding me back from God's promises.

I also have accomplished more in my career since I removed the obstacles blocking the power within me than in the first 20 years of my career. From obtaining my doctorate while successfully leading a global agenda for a top 100 corporation, empowering women through H.E.R.A.C.T. globally, giving back to our community, and being present for our family, my achievements go beyond what I imagined. The achievements are never easy, and there have been many sacrifices. However, God gives me wisdom and strength, and He gives my family peace, love, and joy each time. Yet, nothing brings me more joy than for our children to witness the limitless power of the Holy Spirit that lives in you and me.

We are not free from our life's greatest challenges. Still, each day I have a choice to heal, elevate my mindset, respect my purpose, achieve my fullest potential with confidence based on a spiritual transformation that can only take place through the power of the Holy Spirit. When I walk in the purpose God has destined for me, God takes care of my needs and the needs of our family. In my journey, I have learned my knowledge and capabilities cannot get in the way of the limitless possibilities. Jesus gave us His power as the key to daily living a victorious holistic life. The power is within us, and it is up to us to remove what constricts it.

To fulfill your purpose will take a lifetime. It is a journey you must embrace daily, confident that the infinite power and fire that lives within you has unlocked a limitless potential ready, willing, and able to achieve your purpose.

GLOSSARY

- **Activation energy:** The power needed to push a boulder up a hill onto the other side.
- **Arise:** Emerge, become apparent, come into being.
- **Blind Spot:** An area where a person's view is obstructed.
- **Born Again in Christ:** Means to put our flesh (sin/limitation) to rest so that we can see His promise.
- **Catalyst:** An individual, object, or event that brings about lasting change.
- **Doormat treatment:** When you feel you cannot stand up for yourself and others take advantage.
- **Emotional Quotient:** Also known as EQ, or emotional intelligence.
- **Emotional Intelligence:** Measures an individual's ability to manage emotions.
- **Forgiveness:** Not holding on to someone else's sin.
- **Fruits of the Spirit:** "The fruit of the Spirit is love, joy, peace, longsuffering, kindness, goodness, faithfulness, gentleness, and self-control." Galatians 5:22-23.
- **Healing:** Refers to emotional and spiritual healing.
- **Imposter Syndrome:** Refers to individuals who feel they are a fraud even though they are intelligent people.
- **Innovation antibodies:** Refer to an unhappy employee who effectively shortstops corporate innovation.
- **Leader:** A person who leads or commands. You are the leader of your actions.
- **PERMA Theory:** For over a decade, this theory supports constructive change in positive emotions, engagement, relationships, meaning, and achievement.

- **Prosocial behavior:** Defined by Nancy Eisenborg as voluntary behavior intended to benefit another.
- **Rise:** Gives out a bright light. Very talented. Sees in the darkness.
- **Sanctification:** Refers to the process in which there is no sin separating an individual from God.
- **Shame:** The crushing belief that our past becomes our identity.
- **Self-advocacy:** The action of representing yourself.
- **Self-confidence:** Trust in one's own abilities, qualities, and judgment.
- **Self-efficacy:** The ability to have self-confidence in yourself to succeed.
- **Self-limiting beliefs:** Harmful and inaccurate thoughts about ourselves.
- **Transformation:** A thorough or dramatic change.
- **Trauma:** In this book, relates to the absence of things a woman should have but never received, such as love and positive affirmations. Trauma also refers to the things a woman may have acquired and did not ask for nor deserve, such as mental abuse, criticism, physical abuse, or abandonment.
- **Uninvited guests:** Also known as limiting beliefs.
- **Values:** What you stand for in public and private, regardless of the consequences—a person's principles or standards of behavior; one's judgment of what is important in life.

REFERENCES

- Akhtar, S., Dolan, A., & Barlow, J. (2017). Understanding the relationship between state forgiveness and psychological well-being: A qualitative study. *Journal of Religion and Health,* 56(2), 450-463. doi: http://dx.doi.org.ezproxy.regent.edu/10.1007/s10943-016-0188-9.
- Archer, S. & Yates, J. (2017). Understanding potential career changers' experience of career confidence following a positive psychology-based coaching program. *Coaching: An International Journal of Theory, Research, and Practice,* 10(2), 157-175.
- Argyris, C. (2010). *Organizational Traps, Leadership, Culture, Organizational Design,* Oxford University Press, Oxford, NY.
- Baker, P. & Norton, L. (2019). Fat Loss Forever: How to Lose Fat and Keep it Off. *Biolayne.* 3
- Bandura, A. (1997). *Self-Efficacy: The exercise of control.* Freeman, NY.
- Barsh, J. & Yee, L. (April 2011). Unlocking the full potential of women in the U.S. economy. *McKinsey & Company.*
- Bekker, C.J. (2009). Leading with the Head Bowed Down: Lessons in Leadership Humility from the Rule of St. Benedict of Nursia. *Inner Resources for Leaders,* 1(3), 1-10.
- Bischoff, S.J., DeTienne, K.B., & Quick, B. (1999). Effects of ethics stress on employee burnout and fatigue: An empirical investigation. *Journal of Health and Human Services Administration,* 21(4), 512-532.

- Blackaby, H.T., & Blackaby, R. (2011). *Spiritual leadership: Moving People on to God's agenda.* B&H Publishing Group.
- Bonner, B.L. & Bolinger, A.R. (2013). Separating the confidence from the correct: Leveraging member knowledge in groups to improve decision making and performance. *Organizational Behavior and Human Decision Processes,* 122(2), 214-221. https://doi.org/10.1016/j.obhdp.2013.07.005
- Borowa, D., Kossakowska, M.M., Harmon, K.A., & Robitschek, C. (2018). Personal growth initiative's relation to life meaning and satisfaction in a polish sample: Research and reviews. *Current Psychology,* 1-13. doi: http://dx.doi.org.ezproxy.regent.edu/10.1007/s12144-018-9862-2
- "Bojack Horseman-TV Episode Recaps & News," Vulture, October 30, 2018, accessed February 27, 2021, https://www.vulture.com/tv/bojack-horseman
- Bratton, V.K., Dodd, N.G., & Brown, F.W. (2011). The impact of emotional intelligence on the accuracy of self-awareness and leadership performance. *Leadership & Organization Development Journal,* 32(2), 127-149. doi:10.1108/01437731111112971.
- Breevaart, K., Bakker, A., Hetland, J., Demerouti, E., Olsen, O.K., & Espevik, R. (2014). Daily transactional and transformational leadership and daily employee engagement. *Journal of Occupational and Organizational Psychology,* 87(1), 138-157. doi:10.1111/Joop.12041.
- Burton, L., & Lent, J. (2016). The use of vision boards as a therapeutic intervention. *Journal of Creativity in Mental Health, 11*(1), 52-65.

- Caldwell, C. (2009). Identity, self-awareness, and self-deception: Ethical implications for leaders and organizations: JBE. *Journal of Business Ethics, 90,* 393-406. https://doi.org/10.1007/s10551-010-0424-2

- Caldwell, C., & Hayes, L. A. (2016). Self-efficacy and self-awareness: moral insights to increased leader effectiveness. *Journal of Management Development.*

- Chapman, M. (2020). Courageous leadership–what defines it in the modern organization. *Strategic HR Review, 19*(2), 47-50. doi:10.1108/SHR-01-2020-0001.

- Cheng, J.T., Tracy, J.L., & Henrich, J. (2010). Pride, personality, and the evolutionary foundations of human social status. *Evolution and Human Behavior, 31*(5), 334-347. https://doi.org/10.1016/j.evolhumbehav.2010.02.004

- Chira, S. & Einhorn, C. (2017). How tough is it to change a culture of harassment? Ask women at Ford. *The New York Times, https://www.nytimes. com/interactive/2017/12/19/us/ford-chicago-sexual-harassment.html*

- Clance, P.R. & Imes, S.A. (1978). The imposter phenomenon in high achieving women: Dynamics and therapeutic intervention. *Psychotherapy: Theory, Research & Practice, 15*(3), 241–247. https://doi. org/10.1037/h0086006

- Clark, J. (2015) *The Five Principles of Global Leadership How to Manage the Complexities of Global Leadership.* Bloomington, IN. WestBow Press.

- Coffey, J.K., Wray-lake, L., Mashek, D., & Branand, B.

(2016). A multi-study examination of well-being theory in college and community samples. *Journal of Happiness Studies,* 17(1), 187-211.

- Corrigan, P.W., Bink, A.B., Schmidt, A., Jones, N., & Rüsch, N. (2016). What is the impact of self-stigma? Loss of self-respect and the "why try" effect. Journal of Mental Health (Abingdon, England), 25(1), 10-15. doi:10.3109/0 9638237.2015.1021902.

- Cozolino, L. (2014). *The Neuroscience of Human Relationships: Attachment and the Developing Social Brain (Norton Series on Interpersonal Neurobiology).* United Kingdom: W.W. Norton.

- Crossman, J. (2010). Conceptualizing spiritual Leadership in secular organizational contexts and its relation to transformational, servant, and environmental *Leadership. Leadership & Organization Development Journal,* 31(7), 596-608. doi:10.1108/01437731011079646.

- D'Cruz, J. (2020). Rationalization and self-sabotage. Behavioral and Brain Sciences, 43 doi: http://dx.doi.org. ezproxy.regent.edu/10.1017/S0140525X19002231

- Dickerson, A., & Taylor, M.A. (2000). Self-limiting behavior in women: Self-esteem and self-efficacy as predictors. *Group & Organization Management, 25*(2), 191-210. doi:10.1177/1059601100252006.

- Dweck, C.S. (2008). M*indset: The new psychology of success.* New York, NY: Random House Digital, Inc.

- Editorial CFFP, "Feminist Utopia" in Post-Genocide Rwanda? Dismantling the Narrative Around Women's Political Representation," CFFP, January

26, 2019, I accessed February 27, 2021, https://
centreforfeministforeignpolicy.org/journal/2018/12/18/
feminist-utopia-in-post-genocide-rwanda-dismantling-
the-narrative-around-womens-political-representation

- Elkins, D.N. (2015). *The human elements of psychotherapy: A nonmedical model of emotional healing.* Washington, DC: American Psychological Association.

- Engstrom, T.W. (1976). *The Making of a Christian Leader: How to Develop Management and Human Resources Skills,* Grand Rapids, MI: Zondervan.

- Enright, R.D. & Fitzgibbons, R.P. (2000). *Helping clients forgive; An empirical guide for resolving anger and restoring hope.* Washington, DC: American Psychological Association.

- Fedler, K.D. (2006). *Exploring Christian Ethics Biblical Foundations for Morality.* John Knox Press. Louisville, KY.

- Flade, P., Asplund, J., & Elliot, G. (2015). Employees who use their strengths outperform those who don't. *Gallup News.*

- Freedman, S. & Zarifkar, T. (2016). The psychology of interpersonal forgiveness and guidelines for forgiveness therapy: What therapists need to know to help their clients forgive. *Spirituality in Clinical Practice,* 3(1), 45–58. https://doi-org.ezproxy.regent.edu/10.1037/scp0000087

- Fothergill, E., Guo, J., Howard, L., Kerns, J.C., Knuth, N.D., Brychta, R., Chen, K.Y., Skarulis, M.C., Walter, M., Walter, P.J., & Hall, K.D. (2016). Persistent metabolic adaptation 6 years after "The Biggest Loser"

competition. *Obesity (Silver Spring, Md.)*, 24(8), 1612
1619. https://doi.org/10.1002/oby.21538

- Gabriel, S., Renaud, J.M., & Tippin, B. (2007). When
  I think of you, I feel more confident about me:
  The relational self and self-confidence. *Journal of
  Experimental Social Psychology*, 43(5), 772-779. https://
  doi.org/10.1016/j.jesp.2006.07.004

- Gallo, S., Editor Training Industry, Partners, V., & Gehrke,
  J. (2020, July 27). The Importance of Self-awareness in
  Leadership. Retrieved from https://trainingindustry.com/
  articles/leadership/the-importance-of-self-awareness-in-
  leadership/Garello, M. (2019, April 20). *La negatividad es
  contagiosa: Rodéate de personas que saquen lo mejor
  de ti*. El Estado Digital. https://www.elestadodigital.
  com/2019/04/20/la-negatividad-es-contagiosa-rodeate-
  de-personas-que-saquen-lo-mejor-de-ti/

- Guillén, L., Mayo, M., & Karelaia, N. (2018). Appearing
  self-confident and getting credit for it: Why it may be
  easier for men than women to gain influence at work.
  Human Resource Management, 57(4), 839-854. https://
  onlinelibrary.wiley.com/doi/10.1002/hrm.21857Goleman,
  D. (1994) Emotional Intelligence, Why It Can Matter More
  Than IQ. New York, NY: Bantam Dell.

- Gyertson, D. (2009). *I Believe in the Holy Spirit: One
  Pilgrim's Response to Contemporary Beliefs About and
  Practices Attributed to the Work and Ministry of the Holy
  Spirit*.

- Haden, J. (2017, October 21). A study of 300,000 people
  found living a longer, happier life isn't just about diet,

exercise, or genetics. https://www.businessinsider.com/a-study-of-300000-people-reveals-the-keys-to-a-longer-happier-life-2017-10

- Hamel, G. & Breen, B. (2007). *The future of management.* Boston, Mass: Harvard Business School Press.

- Haapalainen, A. (2016). Spiritual senses as a resource. *Temenos,* 52(2), 289-311. doi:10.33356/temenos.60308.

- Hariri, Ahmad R.1; Bookheimer, Susan Y.1,2; Mazziotta, John C.1 Modulating emotional responses, NeuroReport: January 17, 2000 - Volume 11 - Issue 1. 43-48.

- Hogan, R.H. & Hogan J. (2007). *Hogan Personality Inventory Manual, Third Edition.* Hogan Assessment Systems. Tulsa, OK.

- Hogg, M.A. (2010). *Influence and Leadership.* Fiske, S.T. Gilbert, D.T., & Lindzey, G. (Eds.), *Handbook of Social Psychology* (p. 1166–1207). John Wiley & Sons, Inc. https://doi.org/10.1002/9780470561119.socpsy002031

- Hlupic, V. (2020). Courageous Leadership: Anita Krohn Traaseth, Former CEO of Innovation Norway. *Strategic HR Review,* 19(2), 51-54. doi:10.1108/SHR-11-2019-0082

- Icheku, V. (2011). *Understanding Ethics and Ethical Decision-Making.* Bloomington, IN: Xlibris Corporation.

- Jit, R., Sharma, C.S., & Kawatra, M. (2017). Healing a Broken Spirit: Role of Servant Leadership. Vikalpa: *The Journal for Decision Makers,* 42(2), 80–94. https://journals.sagepub.com/doi/10.1177/0256090917703754

- Kegan, R. & Lahey, L.L. (2009). *Immunity to change: how to overcome it and unlock potential in yourself and your organization.* Boston, MA: Harvard Business Press.

- Kay, K & Shipman, C. (2014). The Confidence Gap. The Atlantic, 14(1), 1-18. Retrieved from: https://www.theatlantic.com/magazine/archive/2014/05/the-confidence-gap/359815/
- Kerns, C.D. (2014). Strengthening Values Centered Leadership; What, Why and How? Graziado Business Review. 7(2). Retrieved from: https://gbr.pepperdine.edu/2010/08/strengthening-values-centered-leadership/
- Kellenberger, J. *Dying to Self and Detachment*, Taylor & Francis Group, 2016. ProQuest Ebook Central, https://ebookcentral-proquest-com.ezproxy.regent.edu/lib/regent-ebooks/detail.action?docID=956308
- Kisiel, C.L., Fehrenbach, T., Torgersen, E., Stolbach, B., Mcclelland, G., Griffin, G., & Burkman, K. (2014). Constellations of interpersonal trauma and symptoms in child welfare: Implications for a developmental trauma framework. *Journal of Family Violence*, 29(1), 1-14. doi: http://dx.doi.org.ezproxy.regent.edu/10.1007/s10896-013-9559-0
- Korn, G. (2021). *Everybody (Else) Is Perfect: How I Survived Hypocrisy, Beauty, Clicks, and Likes*, New York, NY: Atria Books.
- Kosminsky, P. (2017). CBT for grief: Clearing cognitive obstacles to healing from loss. *Journal of Rational-Emotive & Cognitive-Behavior Therapy*, 35(1), 26-37. doi: http://dx.doi.org.ezproxy.regent.edu/10.1007/s10942-016-0241-3
- Kottler, J.A. (2013). *Change: What really leads to lasting personal transformation*. Oxford University Press, Incorporated.

- Kotter, J.P. (2012). *Leading Change with a New Preface by the Author,* Boston, MA: Harvard Business Review Press.
- Kouzes, J.M., & Posner, B.Z. (2007). *The leadership Challenge,* 6th edition, San Francisco, CA: Jossey-Bass.
- Kraemer, H.M. (2011) *From Values to Action: The Four Principles of Values-Based Leadership.* San Francisco, CA: Jossey-Bass.
- Lawson, D. (2008). Transforming Initiatives: Leadership ethics from the Sermon on the Mount. *The Journal of Applied Christian Leadership,* 3(1), 29-46.
- Loehr, J., & Schwartz, T. (2001). The making of a corporate athlete. *Harvard business review,* 79(1), 120-129.
- Logel, C., Hall, W., Page, G.E., & Cohen, G.L. (2019). Why is it so hard to change? The role of self-integrity threat and affirmation in weight loss. European *Journal of Social Psychology,* 49(4), 748–759. https://doi-org.ezproxy.regent.edu/10.1002/ejsp.2536
- Luchies, L.B., Finkel, E.J., McNulty, J.K., & Kumashiro, M. (2010). The doormat effect: When forgiving erodes self-respect and self-concept clarity. *Journal of Personality and Social Psychology,* 98(5), 734–749. https://doi-org.ezproxy.regent.edu/10.1037/a0017838
- Lynn, M.L., Naughton, M.J., & Vanderveen, S. (2009). Faith at work scale (FWS): Justification, development, and validation of a measure of Judaea-Christian religion in the workplace: JBE. *Journal of Business Ethics,* 85(2), 227-243. doi: http://dx.doi.org.ezproxy.regent.edu/10.1007/s10551-008-9767-3

- Markway, G (2018, September 20). Why self confidence is more important than you think. Retrieved February 23, 2021, from https://www.psychologytoday.com/us/blog/shyness-is-nice/201809/why-self-confidence-is-more-important-you-think
- McGregor, H.A., & Elliot, A.J. (2005). The shame of failure: Examining the link between fear of failure and shame. *Personality & Social Psychology Bulletin, 31(2),* 218-231. doi:10.1177/0146167204271420.
- Mackenzie, J. (2018). Knowing yourself and being worth knowing. *Journal of the American Philosophical Association, 4(2),* 243-261. doi: http://dx.doi.org.ezproxy.regent.edu/10.1017/apa.2018.19
- Madden, A., & Bailey, C. (2017). Engagement. *Organizational Dynamics, 46(2),* 113. doi:10.1016/j.orgdyn.2017.04.007.
- Mann PhD., T. (2015). Secrets From the Eating Lab: The Science of Weight Loss, the Myth of Willpower, and Why You Should Never Diet Again. *HarperCollins.* 163.
- Markey, C., & Gillen, M. (2015;2016;). *Body image and mental health, Encyclopedia of Mental Health,* Elsevier Science & Technology, 2015. *ProQuest Ebook Central,* http://ebookcentral.proquest.com/lib/regent-ebooks/detail.action?docID=4003864
- Created from regent-ebooks on 2021-01-12 08:00:36.
- Maxwell, J.C. (1999). *The 21 Indispensable Qualities of a Leader, Becoming the Person Others Will Want to Follow. Nashville,* TN. Thomas Nelson, Inc.
- McNicol, B., Willard, D., Thrall, B., Matthews, K., Fuller,

P., Demarest, B., & Glerup, M. (2016). *The kingdom life: A practical theology of discipleship and spiritual formation.* Tyndale House Publishers, Inc.

- Morse, G. (2006). Decisions and desire. *Harvard Business Review,* 84(1), 42. Retrieved from: https://hbr.org/2006/01/decisions-and-desire

- Mulholland, M.R., Jr. (1993). *Invitation to a journey: A road map for spiritual formation.* Downers Grove, IL. InterVarsity.

- Muto, S. (2014) *Virtues, Your Christian Legacy.* Steubenville, OH: Emmaus Road Publishing.

- Northouse, P.J. (2016). *Leadership Theory and Practice, 7th edition,* Oaks, CA: Sage Publications, Inc.

- Oster, G. (2011) *The Light Prize Perspectives on Christian Innovation.* Virginia Beach, VA: Positive Signs Media.

- Oster, G. (2009). Listening to Luddites: Innovation Antibodies and Corporate Success. *Revista de Management Comparat Internaţional,* 10(4), 647-667.

- Oexle, N., Müller, M., Kawohl, W., Xu, Z., Viering, S., Wyss, C., ... Rüsch, N. (2018). Self-stigma as a barrier to recovery: A longitudinal study. *European Archives of Psychiatry and Clinical Neuroscience,* 268(2), 209-212. doi: http://dx.doi.org.ezproxy.regent.edu/10.1007/s00406-017-0773-2

- Oswald, A.J., Proto, E., & Sgroi, D. (2015). Happiness and productivity. *Journal of Labor Economics,* 33(4), 789-822.

- Pépin, C. (2019). Self-Confidence: A Philosophy. United States: Other Press, LLC.

- Peterson, E.H. (2006). *East this Book, Study Guide.* Grand Rapids, MI: Wm. B. Eerdmans Publishing Co.

- Phillips, J.J., & Phillips, P.P. (2020). Courageous leadership: Delivering results in turbulent times. *Strategic HR Review, 19*(2), 59-66. doi:10.1108/SHR-01-2020-0002.
- Popova, M. (2014). Fixed vs. Growth: The two basic mindsets that shape our lives. *Brain Pickings.*
- Publishing, H. (n.d.). More evidence that exercise can boost mood. Retrieved from https://www.health.harvard.edu/mind-and-mood/more-evidence-that-exercise-can-boost-mood
- Ravelli, D., Protti, S., & Albini, A. (2015). Energy and molecules from photochemical/photocatalytic reactions. An overview. *Molecules (Basel, Switzerland), 20*(1), 1527-1542. https://doi.org/10.3390/molecules20011527
- Reave, L. (2005). Spiritual values and practices related to leadership effectiveness. *The Leadership Quarterly, 16*(5), 655-687. doi:10.1016/j.leaqua.2005.07.003.
- Reed, G.L., & Enright, R.D. (2006). The effects of forgiveness therapy on depression, anxiety, and posttraumatic stress for women after spousal emotional abuse. *Journal of Consulting and Clinical Psychology, 74*(5), 920–929. https://doi-org.ezproxy.regent.edu/10.1037/0022-006X.74.5.920
- Reich, B. (2017) (Ed.) The Imagination Gap, *Emerald Publishing Limited,* pp. i-xxiv. https://doi.org/10.1108/978-1-78714-206-020171013.
- Rocklage, M.D., Pietri, E.S., & Fazio, R.H. (2017). The weighting of positive vs. negative valence and its impact on the formation of social relationships. *Journal of Experimental Social Psychology, 73,* 65-75. doi:10.1016/j.jesp.2017.06.011.

- Romppel M., Herrmann-lingen C., Wachter R., et al. (2013) A short form of the General Self-Efficacy Scale (GSE-6). Psychosoc Med. 2013;10:Doc01. doi:10.3205/psm000091.
- Sakulku, J. (1). The Impostor Phenomenon. The Journal of Behavioral Science, 6(1), 75-97. https://doi.org/10.14456/ijbs.2011.6
- Scazzero, P. (2015). *The emotionally healthy leader: How transforming your inner life will deeply transform your church, team, and the world.* Grand Rapids, MI: Zondervan.
- Schneider, W.E. (2000). Why good management ideas fail. *Strategy & Leadership,* 28(1), 24-29. doi:10.1108/10878570010336001.
- Seligman, M. (2011). PERMA-V: *Our framework for well-being.* Retrieved December 30, 2020, from https://www.stac.school.nz/why-stac/well-being-at-stac/perma-v/
- Seligman, Dr. M. (2020) *Authentic Happiness,* Penn University of Pennsylvania Positive Psychology Center. Retrieved from: https://www.authentichappiness.sas.upenn.edu/learn
- Sias, P.M., & Bartoo, H. (2007). Friendship, social support, and health. In *Low-cost approaches to promote physical and mental health* (pp. 455-472). Springer, New York, NY.
- Singh, D. (2006) *Emotional Intelligence at Work, A Professional Guide.* Thousand Oaks, CA: Response Books.
- Shuck, B., & Reio, T.G. (2014). Employee engagement and well-being: A moderation model and implications for practice. *Journal of Leadership & Organizational Studies,* 21(1), 43-58. doi:10.1177/1548051813494240.

- Steger, M.F., Frazier, P., Oichi, S., & Kaler, M. (2006). The meaning in life questionnaire: Assessing the presence of and search for meaning in life. *Journal of Counseling Psychology*, 53(1), 80–93. https://doi.org/10.1037/0022-0167.53.1.80.

- Sun, J., Liden, R.C., & Ouyang, L. (2019). Are servant leaders appreciated? An investigation of how relational attributions influence employee feelings of gratitude and prosocial behaviors. *Journal of Organizational Behavior*, 40(5), 528-540. doi:10.1002/job.2354.

- Sweden's Maternity and Paternity Leave," Yale School of Public Health, June 01, 2018, I accessed February 27, 2021, https://publichealth.yale.edu/news-article/17486/

- Theodores, D. (2020). The 3 Cs of courageous leadership: How to connect to your body, connect to your creativity, connect to your inner revolutionary. *Strategic HR Review*, 19(2), 81-83. doi:10.1108/SHR-04-2020-177.

- The health benefits of good friends. (2019, August 24). Retrieved January 08, 2021, from https://www.mayoclinic.org/healthy-lifestyle/adult-health/in-depth/friendships/art-20044860

- Tomova, L., von Dawans, B., Heinrichs, M., Silani, G., & Lamm, C. (2014). Is stress affecting our ability to tune into others? Evidence for gender differences in the effects of stress on self-other distinction. *Psychoneuroendocrinology*, 43, 95-104. doi:10.1016/j.psyneuen.2014.02.006.

- Transcripts Whitney Houston: Her Life, Her Music. (2012, February 18). CNN Transcripts. http://transcripts.cnn.com/TRANSCRIPTS/1202/18/se.03.html

- Văcar, A. (2015). Influence And Leadership, *Studies in Business and Economics*, 10(2), 196-201. doi: https://doi.org/10.1515/sbe-2015-0030

- Van Velsor, E.V., McCauley, C.D., & Ruderman, M.N. (Eds.), 2010. *The Center for Creative Leadership Handbook of Leadership Development* (3rd Ed.) San Francisco, CA. Jossey-Bass.

- Velez, B.L., Campos, I.D., & Moradi, B. (2015). Relations of sexual objectification and racist discrimination with Latina Women's body image and mental health. *The Counseling Psychologist*, 43(6), 906-935. doi:10.1177/0011000015591287.

- Vijayaraghavan, K. (2015, Feb 09). Why staying fit is imperative for business heads getting older & seeking to stay at the top [panache]. *The Economic Times* Retrieved from http://eres.regent.edu/login?url=https://www-proquest-com.ezproxy.regent.edu/newspapers/why-staying-fit-is-imperative-business-heads/docview/1652273454/se-2?accountid=13479

- Vujanovic, A.A., Hart, A.S., Potter, C.M., Berenz, E.C., Niles, B., & Bernstein, A. (2013). Main and interactive effects of distress tolerance and negative affect intensity in relation to PTSD symptoms among trauma-exposed adults. *Journal of Psychopathology and Behavioral Assessment*, 35(2), 235-243. doi: http://dx.doi.org.ezproxy.regent.edu/10.1007/s10862-012-9325-2

- Warner, G. "It's The No. 1 Country For Women In Politics—But Not In Daily Life," NPR, July 29, 2016, accessed February 27, 2021, https://www.npr.org/sections/goatsandsoda/2016/07/29/487360094/invisibilia-no-one-thought-this-all-womans-debate-team-could-crush-it)

- Weiss, T (2014). Personal transformation: Posttraumatic growth and gerotranscendence. *The Journal of Humanistic Psychology,* 54(2), 203-226. https://doi.org/10.1177/0022167813492388
- Yafang, T. (2011). Relationship between Organizational Culture, Leadership Behavior and Job Satisfaction. *BMC Health Services Research,* 11(1), 98-106. doi:10.1186/1472-6963-11-98.

About the Author

Dr. Merary Simeon is an activator of talent with a mission to create a world where multicultural women in positions of power are the norm. She is a community-minded, people-invested, and kingdom work advocate. Dr. Simeon is a proven and celebrated human resources executive with over 25 years of experience working for Fortune 100 companies.

Dr. Simeon's diverse experiences have equipped her with a deep understanding of the needs and opportunities critical to leaders at all levels. She has led dispersed professional teams across the US and Latin America. She is a trusted thought partner to the C-suite and continuously demonstrates the ability to lead change and integrate initiatives cross-functionally. She is known for her strategic thinking, delivering results, motivating teams, and exceeding expectations. Dr. Simeon has extensive experience in Talent Management, Executive Coaching, Change Management, Organizational Design, Diversity, Equity & Inclusion, Selection & Succession Planning, Content Development, Labor Relations, and Public Speaking.

Dr. Simeon is also a best-selling book author and a non-profit board member. She holds a doctorate in strategic leadership. She is the co-founder of Color Forward and Co-host of What Rules!? Podcast. She credits her success to Jesus Christ. She is a native of Puerto Rico and lives in Texas with her family.

www.merarysimeon.com
merary@merarysimeon.com
linkedin.com/merarysimeon

Made in the USA
Coppell, TX
15 September 2022

83196349R00118